Thoughts To Live By

Thoughts To Live By

Maxwell Maltz, M.D., F.I.C.S.

Thought Works Books
A Division of Micro Publishing Media

Thoughts To Live By
Copyright © 2022 Matt Furey

All rights reserved. This book or any portion thereof may not be reproduced or used in any manner whatsoever without the express written permission of the publisher except for the use of brief quotations in a book review.

This book is a classic reprint of a manuscript written when some phrases and societal norms would conflict with those of today. To avoid confusion, we have kept the original references to gender roles, but the book is written to be inclusive. The editors have made every effort to remove offensive language while maintaining the essence of Dr. Maltz's original message and wording.

Printed in the United States of America

ISBN xx-xxx-xxxxx

Thought Works Books

A division of Micro Publishing Media, Inc
PO Box 1522
Stockbridge, MA 01262

www.thoughtworksbooks.com

Everyone was born to succeed, Dr. Maltz believes. Everyone has a marvelous creative potential that can be discovered and used for a happier, more productive life.

Out of a rich and useful life, he offers you the wisdom gained through many years of study, observation, and medical practice. He is a practical, reassuring book that will help you discover your self-image, expand it, and thereby expand your potential for living. Here are the simple principles that have helped millions toward self-fulfillment, even in a confusing and troubled world.

This classic reprint is as relevant today as when it was first published in 1975. The second part of the original book had a list of 366 inspirational quotes, one for each day of the year and one extra for leap year. We decided to create a separate calendar book with some additional inspirations, images and goal setting activities. You can find it at www.maxwellmaltzbooks.com

Preface

I was first introduced to the teachings of Dr. Maxwell Maltz in May of 1987. At the time I was just starting out in business as a fitness trainer, and one of my first clients, Jack, a successful real estate broker, asked me if I had read *Psycho-Cybernetics*.

After telling Jack that I hadn't read it, I asked for more information. He proceeded to tell me that **Psycho-Cybernetics** was "the Bible of self-development."

As soon as our session ended, I drove to the bookstore and picked up a copy and began reading. I was absolutely enthralled with the timeless message in the book and couldn't stop thinking about how it applied to my life.

Upon finishing the book, I looked for everything I could find that was written by Dr. Maltz. Over the next month, I bought every book I could find that had Dr. Maltz' name on it, and I spent every spare moment studying his teachings and applying them to my life.

Little did I know or imagine at the time, that I would eventually become the heir to the Maltz library and business, that I would be involved in an updated and expanded version of *Psycho-Cybernetics*, that I would be coaching and consulting with business executives, salespeople, doctors, lawyers, teachers, coaches and world-class athletes, passing on the amazing and life-transforming teachings of self-image psychology.

As one thought and action lead to another, my fascination with Dr. Maltz' teachings took another turn for the better when I began a co-venture with Deborah Herman of Thought Works Books. With her help, we are keeping the Maltz legacy alive by publishing the good doctor's books that have inexplicably fallen out of the public eye, or that needed to a slight refreshing.

If you loved *Psycho-Cybernetics,* I am certain you will adore the other books that Dr. Maltz wrote and that Thought Works Books is now publishing. When you apply Dr. Maltz' words of wisdom, you will discover, as I did, that they are timeless because they are true. You can apply his principles at any age and for virtually any endeavor. I began benefitting from his advice straight out of college, and I'm still doing so today.

Enjoy this book... and all the others in the Maltz library and watch as your life continues to grow and expand in any and all areas that are important to you.

Matt Furey
President of The Psycho-Cybernetics Foundation
Psycho-Cybernetics.com

Introduction

Descartes said, "I think, therefore I am." How important are these five words to you? They should be the most important five words in your life, every minute, every hour, every day, every week, every month, every year. These words are your passport to happiness. You can travel wherever you choose, and you will never be alone. With these words, you create a worthwhile foundation in the world within your mind and heart, a world of light and calm and order. These five words separate you from the animal; they are the keys to the greatness within you that is awaiting recognition.

What a terrible world this would be if we didn't think. Of course, Descartes meant constructive, not destructive, thinking, using your thoughts not to hurt others, or to aggressively step on others, or to destroy yourself with negative thoughts. Descartes didn't mean thinking uncertainty, despair, fear, insecurity, loneliness, resentment, and emptiness, all corroding factors in negative thinking.

If you can grasp the true meaning of these five words, you will have the keys to achievement and happiness. You will be able to live constructively in a creative world, having the power to do your thing productively, understanding your own needs and the needs of others. You can learn to use your courage, self-respect, self-acceptance, and self-confidence to make these five words mean what they really do. We, in the present day, go a little further. We say, "I think, therefore I am... and I *do!*" You reach fulfillment when you not only think creatively but act creatively to reach worthwhile goals. This is what Psycho-Cybernetics means: clear, constructive thinking, steering your mind to a productive, useful goal.

You will find in the pages of this book something that will help you on your way to self-fulfillment.

By self-fulfillment, I mean more than the financial security you deserve. I mean finding more meaning to your life, whatever your age, getting more living out of life—something you must achieve for yourself.

To help you in your successful evolution, I have written 366 Capsule Thoughts to Live By in a separate book with inspirations and a place to write your goals. It is my hope that on each day of the year, you will build your better self-image by elaborating on each capsule thought writing essays of a page or two similar to the ones in the book. This companion book will help you crystalize and maintain a blueprint for a brighter future.

You are embarking on the greatest adventure of your life, to improve your self-image, to create more meaning in your life and in the lives of others. This is your responsibility. Accept it now!

Courage

These are the words on courage by Cervantes:

He that loses wealth loses much:
But he that loses courage loses all.

Courage, like compassion, is one of the great ingredients of the success instinct in man. I cannot imagine anyone being a successful human being without courage, without the capacity to overcome obstacles and reach a constructive goal, without the fortitude to cling to ideals that encompass good for him and for his brothers and sisters the world over.

Courage is the outward expression of the three worlds in which man lives—his physical world, his mental world, and his spiritual world.

Courage—I mean creative courage—of necessity implies the search for freedom on these three levels, which in turn means the search for truth for good.

Courage that demands that you stand up for your rights and the rights of others, the kind of glorious courage that built our nation; courage to live with compassion, not aggression; courage to live in belief, not doubt; courage to live in hope, not despair; courage to surmount crises instead of being overwhelmed by them; courage to build self-reliance; courage to accept a mistake instead of rebuking yourself for not being perfect—these are true aspects of courage! Remember, although you are an island within yourself, you belong to the mainland with others and are destined to share your courage with others.

Keep Going

Columbus, as he sailed across the uncharted routes of the Atlantic, not knowing where he was going, wrote in his private log, "This day we sailed on course WSW." Surely, he must have been filled with hope and faith that he was headed right, that he would reach his destination. Surely, too, he must have had thoughts of despair that he would never reach his goal, that he might flounder endlessly on angry waters, perhaps lost forever to the world. Things couldn't have been worse. His ships were damaged, and the men were threatening mutiny. Did he at times lose his hope and faith and confidence? Of course he did!

But in moments of despair, frustration, and crisis, Columbus called upon his courage. He knew he had to be right, and he kept on going. Why? Because he had inner integrity. Have you integrity during a period of distress? Have you self-respect during crises? Do you call upon your confidence in desperate moments of despair and futility, in panic, when you are lost in the rough seas of frustration? Unable to reach port? Threatening mutiny on yourself? Greatness exists when you are trying to be great. When? At a time of crisis. At a time of doubt, distress, and despair, are you willing to write on a slip of paper the words of Columbus, "This day we sailed on," and then live by them? It is your moral responsibility to do so.

The Great Balance

Here is a couplet written in 1591 by John Florio:

When you are an anvil, hold you still;
When you are a hammer, strike your fill

Life is the great balance between the anvil and the hammer. The eternal struggle between failure and success, between hope and despair, between joy and sorrow. We all have our terrifying feelings of loneliness and despair, and they can strike at any hour, at any moment. Creative living teaches us that under these circumstances, we brace ourselves against the stress, against the shock. These are our anvil moments.

But then we have our hammer moments. With hope and faith within us, there comes a time when we can perform, when we can reach goals and contribute to life, when we can prove by action that we are willing to put our integrity on the line for minorities who are abused. We can really prove that we understand our own needs and the needs of others. We can utilize our confidence creatively to find success and share it with others. We can live in the sunny present instead of the foggy past. Then we are the spiritual hammer. With resolution and determination, we can strike hard at the right place. We can strive for the right goal within our capabilities and forge the big self that we can be, that we are, remembering always to share this bigness of self with other people.

Praise

What is praise? it is a varied expression of love and friendship, and we should use it more often to compliment someone for a deed well done, for a word well spoken. Why be effusive in our praise of someone when he is put to rest in a cemetery and can't hear a word of it?

What is praise? Something we all need now and then. Every human being, whether he is a beggar or a tycoon, a peasant or a philosopher, a student or a teacher, whether he is alone or married, searches desperately for recognition. One of the greatest goals for every human being is to feel needed, wanted for something somewhere. We deserve this praise not when we demand it or search for it, but when we receive it naturally in the process of doing something for others, while we are doing something for ourselves.

Since my book *Psycho-Cybernetics* was published in 1959, 1 have received thousands of letters from people all over the world thanking me for helping them to be themselves, for making them feel they are needed. We all need each other, and we should make it our business to praise when necessary. Remember, love and friendship are priceless at any age.

Consider the words of Berton Braley:

If you think that praise is due him,
Now's the time to slip it to him,
For he cannot read his tombstone when he's dead.

On Pettiness

Disraeli said, "Life is too short to be little." Seven words! We should remember these words every moment of every day. "Life is too short to be little." Think about the horrors of war that man has not been able to stop since the beginning of time. Think what has happened in the last fifty years! The advances in medicine and other sciences, landings on the moon, progress toward the cure of cancer, our youth evolving, despite their mistakes, to a greatness that will make this place a better world. We are coming closer and closer to the brotherhood of man.

Every human being has a divine instinct within him to contribute to this new world of greatness through the assets within him: understanding, self-respect, courage, forgiveness, self-acceptance, and self-confidence. Nor should we overlook compassion, which eventually will bring about the peace we so fervently desire.

Under these circumstances, how can one be petty? Suppose we are all that way now and then because we are very fragile and easily hurt. But why not use our inner strength to rise above petty hurts, the pettiness of rancor, jealousy, and envy when the world is asking us, pleading with us to be big with understanding, friendship, and love? Let us devote our lives to worthwhile goals, to creative achievement, to happiness and we won't have to be told to share this happiness with others. We will! We know that life is too short to be petty.

On Imagination

The poet William Blake wrote these lines:

To see a world in a grain of sand,
And heaven in a wildflower,
Hold infinity in the palm of your hand,
And eternity in an hour.

These words describe so clearly the power of the imagination. Do you think that only musicians, poets, artists, and dramatists, those who work through experience to create beauty, have imagination? If you do, you are wrong.

We are all blessed with the power of a creative imagination. A boy of six, with other young students, was studying words ending in "ll" in a school in St. Louis. When they came to the word "kill," he said, "We shouldn't study this word in school. Why don't we put the letter 's' in front of it?" At six, he turned the word "kill" into "skill!" He showed that he could use his imagination creatively, not only for himself but for the whole world.

In these times of violence, when a human being sometimes feels he is worth nothing, the beauty of imagination is lost, hidden, suppressed. The rapid pace in which we live tends to warp the free play of the imagination. But you, all of us, have imagination just as you have self-respect. You cannot ignore your imagination any more than your self-respect if you are to survive in creative terms. It is our human responsibility every day to reclaim our imagination and to see the beauty within us and around us.

The Happiness Principle

The happiness principle, in simple terms, means this: The more you share your happiness with others, the more you have yourself. It also means that the happier you are, the wiser you are. And, finally, happiness is good, just as unhappiness is evil. When you are happy, the glorious things in nature are more visible: the flowers smell better, the sound of a rippling brook is more distinct, food tastes better, the hand of friendship is firmer, and your voice has more life to it. On the other hand, when you are unhappy, you cannot see the beauty without and within: you don't hear as well as you could, nothing smells right, the food doesn't taste good, your touch is benumbed, and your voice is lost in loneliness. Happiness is internal. It means clear perception within you, where you see the possibilities of becoming bigger and better than you are for yourself and for others. It means sharing your good fortune with others who need your good will desperately. In unhappiness, your spiritual vision is clouded by a mental cataract so that you cannot see the good in yourself; you cannot be kind to yourself or wise enough to realize that loneliness and fear are your blind spots. Remember the words of John Masefield, the famous poet laureate of England: "The days that make us happy make us wise."

Arrival

Cervantes, the great author of *Don Quixote,* said, "The road is always better than the inn." If you think about these words for a moment, you will discover that they represent a glorious and productive way of living.

In my younger days, when, like anyone else, I was after my goal, I believed that when I reached it, I would find satisfaction and a reward for my achievement. But soon, I realized that we are all goal strivers; and when we reach one goal, we must start for another goal the next day. In other words, each goal achieved is like an inn. It is merely a temporary resting place along the road, the endless road of self-fulfillment. Creative living means motion, movement, turning away from dead ends as you move along the highway to achievement. The great fun and pleasure are the journey, because it is your area of creative effort. The joy of a great painter is more in the creation of a painting than in the final display of it in a gallery. I have always kept moving on various highways toward the operating room, toward the writing of a book, toward medical research in wound healing, toward the lecture platform. Only then could I look back to the joys of accomplishment and look forward with hope, desire, belief, and determination to a new tomorrow. Each inn of today is a stopping point for a moment; but in reality, it is a starting point for a new adventure. And this road that we travel is all the more beautiful if, at the same time, we travel within the world of mind and spirit, making sure that the dead ends of negative feelings are not there. The great expectation of self-fulfillment improves the prospect of your greatest achievement.

An Inside Job

When we speak of an inside job, we usually mean a carefully contrived crime executed by "people in the know." If a bank is robbed and there are no clues, it might be an inside job. If a home is rifled, with valuable jewelry missing, and the theft was executed with neat dispatch, no complications, we ask ourselves if this crime was not an inside job. The most pernicious kind of inside job is the crime we inflict upon ourselves when, through fear or hatred, we rob ourselves of peace of mind by persisting in endless self-criticism. Indeed, we create prison walls around ourselves, preventing achievement of happiness. Are you an "inside jobber" who walks away from reality into the gloomy tunnels of a disturbed mind? Do you hurl yourself into a dungeon of futility?

If you do, do not despair, because Psycho-Cybernetics is an inside job, a creative inside job. You can change. Psycho-Cybernetics will do an inside job that will 'unprove' your self-image and help you to grow in stature as a professional human being. This creative inside job will bolster your belief in yourself as you rise above mistakes to self-respect and compassion. You must refuse to make a mountain out of a mole hill, performing daily tasks without pressure. What is your inside job? To use your creative mechanism for success, not failure, achieving your position as a professional human being.

On Enthusiasm

Enthusiasm is one of our most important traits and assets that keeps us young whether we are three, thirty, six, sixty, nine, or ninety. This means that people of all ages can find eternal youth within or without if they have an eagerness to fulfill themselves. Everyone has enthusiasm, whether they are aware of it or not, simply because enthusiasm is within each of us, waiting to be utilized for creative performance and reaching a productive goal.

You must find your enthusiasm. Like confidence and like opportunity, you must create it for yourself without waiting for someone to thrust it upon you. In other words, no one can make you enthusiastic without your consent. No one can make you eager to achieve goals without your consent.

Enthusiasm is a thought turned into a performance; it is the kinetic energy that propels you to your destination. But first, you must have a goal you want to achieve. Enthusiasm implies that you believe in yourself, that you concentrate with courage, that you return to your big self to complete a job, that you practice self-discipline, that you have a dream, that you see victory in the distance. You will reach your goal if you use your imagination, grow daily in stature, and adjust to realities while you yearn for improvement.

Can you find enthusiasm with doubt, despair, fear, frustration, worry, or distrust? Of course not. These negative feelings tell you that you are getting old before your time, just as enthusiasm tells you that you can be young and successful as long as you want.

In the words of Ralph Waldo Emerson, "Nothing great was ever achieved without enthusiasm."

The Stranger Within

You meet strangers every day of your life wherever you go. But did it ever occur to you that you, yourself, do not go alone, that there is a stranger who keeps you company all the time. This stranger is close to you, closer than a wife, or a child, or a parent, or a friend. It is the stranger within you. The reason it is a stranger is that you don't know him. You are unaware of his presence, unaware of what his function is. It is important that you get to know him better, because if you do, he can become your best friend. To be truly happy, you must be sincere with this stranger. If you ignore him or don't understand him, he may become your worst enemy.

Do you know that you have a self-image behind your face? This self-image symbolically has a face of its own; it is the face of your mind that dominates your life. It is your inner Siamese twin from which you can't escape. This twin controls your life because, whether you realize it or not, you do what it tells you.

This self-image, then, is the stranger within you. It is the heartbeat of your mind, the built-in clock that ticks away the hours of happiness or sorrow, depending on your understanding of him. Your self-image is your emotional thermostat that regulates your behavior to others and to yourself. This stranger, your self-image, is the opinion you have of yourself and is made up of your successes and failures in life. If you are overcome by failures of the past as you try to cope with your daily goal in the present, you are filled with unbelief that distorts and disfigures your self-image. You are then ashamed of this self-image, and you limit yourself in your capabilities through worry and fear.

If you take advantage of your successes of the past, you use belief, courage, and self-confidence for present undertakings. This enhances your self-image. The stranger within you then becomes your best friend, who now encourages you to reach your true stature of dignity and fulfillment.

The most important point to remember is that this stranger within doesn't rule you. You rule him. Rule him creatively, with compassion, and you will get more living out of life. Here is a thought to live by: Napoleon said, "None but myself did me any harm."

Your Best Face

The story is told of an adviser of President Lincoln who recommended a candidate for the Lincoln cabinet. Lincoln declined, and when asked why, he said, "I don't like the man's face." "But the poor man is not responsible for his face," his adviser insisted. "Every man over forty is responsible for his face," Lincoln replied, and the subject was dropped.

Are you responsible for your face? I believe so; but as a plastic surgeon, I feel we must exclude persons whose faces are scarred as a result of accidents at home, on the highway, and in industry, and children born with disfigurements. These people are responsible for their faces once they are brought back to normal.

What Lincoln really meant was this. Every human being is responsible for his face after forty because forty years of living should put a great deal into a face—the joys, the sorrows, the struggles for survival, the mistakes, the heartaches, the feeling of loneliness and despair, and the determination to surmount problems. As a result of these emotional and spiritual upheavals, people become wiser, gentler, more compassionate. They are able to understand their own needs and the needs of others. They are able to show kindness and sympathy, a willingness to erase resentment, hatred, bigotry, and to stand up to uncertainty and loneliness. Under these circumstances, when you find the big you, it doesn't matter ff there is a wrinkle on your face. It is not on the face of your mind. Shakespeare said, "To thine own self be true." We say, "To thine own self-image be true," and you will show the world your best face at all times.

What Are You Becoming?

Recently someone asked me what is hope? I said hope is our guide to the future. In these violent times, any of us wonder what will become of the human race. That depends on what becomes of each human being. And that, in the final analysis, depends on what each person wants out of life.

Socrates said, "Know thyself." Marcus Aurelius said, "Be thyself." Shakespeare said, "To thine own self be true." I believe it goes further. Every day you must rethink who you are. Every day you must adjust your self-image to the changing conditions of the day. Your image, your opinion of yourself, and the road map of where you are going in life are never static. You are in motion, moving toward a goal, even while you are asleep; because even while you sleep, your success mechanism is at work subconsciously. You think in creative terms of reaching your true stature of self-respect.

It is not so much what your image is but what you are doing with it creatively this very minute. It is not so much who you are as what you are becoming each day: growing, doing, rethinking, redoing, regrowing. The hope of mankind lies in what you are becoming by doing, giving, sharing, growing, by honoring your own integrity and the self-respect of others. This is the only way to remove hate and evil, the only way to become a successful human being.

What are you becoming this very minute? You are becoming the creative you, adding more years to your life and more life to your years. Say to yourself every day as long as you live, "This is the first day of the best of my life," and prove it by living it.

Simplicity

Ralph Waldo Emerson said, "Nothing is more simple than greatness, Indeed, to be simple is to be great."

Yes, I believe that every human being is great when he lives a life of simplicity, refusing to be tied down by the countless weight of details and nit-picking.

Simplicity should be a goal for every human being, because through it, one can move toward his destination without being sidetracked by dead ends that prevent us from becoming our big selves.

You live the rules of simplicity when you get rid of the pollution within your mind today, now, when you get rid of the resentments that inevitably complicate your existence. Simplicity also means one goal at a time. It means that you must stop criticizing yourself and others. It means doing what you cannot trying to imitate or to be someone else.

It means seeing life every day as it is, not dreaming what it should be. Simplicity means peace of mind, and where do you find it? Within you, not thousands of miles away on a Sunny island in the Pacific. What do you want out of life? Do you want ostentation that winds up making your image ten inches small, or do you want simplicity that gives you inner security and makes your image ten feet tall?

Remember the words of Henry Thoreau, "Our life is frittered away by detail. Simplify, simplify."

Failure

We all, now and then, fail in some undertaking. This gives us feelings of uncertainty, feelings of insecurity. Some of us are ashamed of failure and let past failures rule our lives. We do so at a time when we are trying to reach a worthwhile goal in the present; but we deter ourselves from this goal by worrying about past failures that make us fearful we will fail again in our present undertaking.

I remember, when I was a premedical student at Columbia University, I failed organic chemistry and feared that I would never become a doctor. But my desire to be a doctor was so great that I took the chemistry course during the summer, studied hard, and passed with an "A." I rose above failure because I had a goal, a goal important to me.

Success in life means not only to succeed but to rise above failures. We have a Failure Mechanism within us made up of past defeats, and the elements of this Failure Mechanism are:

1. Fear
2. Anger
3. Inferiority
4. Loneliness
5. Uncertainty
6. Resentment
7. Emptiness

If we are overcome by these elements of the Failure Mechanism, we walk away from life because we neglect our assets, our built-in Success Mechanism. Failure leads to tension, corrosion, a lack of belief.

We must learn to accept ourselves for what we are. We are never perfect. We will likely make mistakes that distort our self-image, but we must learn to have courage to profit by these mistakes and not to be sidetracked by them in our present undertakings. Rising above failure results in confidence, and failure has tremendous value; it stimulates us to rise above it.

The greatest failure of all is to be afraid to make a mistake, to be afraid to take the calculated risk of living and improving ourselves. If we rise above this fear, we automatically enhance our self-image, and this is bound to bring the happiness we seek.

Remember the words of Thomas Bailey Aldrich, "They fail, and they alone, who have not striven."

This Is Your Life

This is your life, and you've got to find somebody. You've got to find somebody very important—your big self. This is your life, and it's far too short to waste any moment of it making yourself less than what you are. This is your life, and it urges you to live in the present, to do one thing at a time. Stop criticizing others and yourself. See the sun around you and within you. Find the good in you and in others. Have compassion for yourself and for others. Refuse to be petty and resentful; refuse to hurt others and yourself.

This is your life. Live it to the fullest without stepping on other people's toes, without stepping on your own toes through negative feelings. This is your life. Refuse to merely exist; live creatively. You do when you redeem yourself, when you come back to your true worth, when you give yourself another chance and another chance.

You will give yourself another chance when you concentrate with courage on what you have to do, when you retrieve the good in you, when you listen to others, trying to help them, when you aspire for yourself and for others, when you try and keep trying, when you encourage others, thereby encouraging yourself, when you adjust to the realities of every day, taking the good with the bad, when you yearn for improvement, making that your daily goal in life.

This is your life, and you must find your big self. Believe me, you can!

How To Jump A Hurdle

I know a hurdle champion who won many medals at college. Very few could beat him. He was the epitome of grace, agility, and fast footwork. He had numerous friends who admired him for his athletic prowess, and one of them gave the champ a job as a salesman in his insurance company. Years passed. He got married, and now he has a five-year-old son. But somehow, he never went far in his field as a salesman. He was likable, made friends easily, but could sell only a small amount of insurance during a year. He didn't seem to have the drive, the courage, the perseverance, or the great desire to achieve the perfection he achieved in hurdle jumping. Fear that he would not be a perfect salesman overcame him, distorted his self-image. He was easily frustrated when he was turned down by a potential customer. He forgot that he overcame mistakes in hurdling when he was at college by practice and perseverance.

One day at a class reunion at college, he met his classmates. They spent some time on the field. Some students were practicing jumping the hurdles. His friends coaxed him to see how good he remained. He had a drink or two in him. He borrowed a pair of sneakers and rushed to jump the hurdles, remembering how good he was in the past. He slipped and broke his leg. He was in a cast for a month, and this gave him time to think, to take stock of himself.

He recalled that he became a champ through constant practice, by overcoming failures. He realized that he was much too old for hurdle jumping; but he remembered that when he was a student, he had self-confidence and understanding of his skill. He also remembered courage, self-respect, self-acceptance. He recalled that he had a sense of direction when he jumped the hurdles toward his goal. He suddenly realized that there was no reason on earth he couldn't be a champion salesman. Why couldn't he jump the hurdles of life, why couldn't he jump the hurdles of his job, why couldn't he do better? He knew that fear and lack of confidence kept him from being a champion.

When he got well, he approached selling insurance with the same understanding, the same tenacity that he had applied to hurdle jumping. He practiced in his mind how to approach his customer and how to overcome possible obstacles. In less than a year, he became a top-flight salesman, increased his earning capacity, and was very happy.

We, too, can jump the hurdles of tension and stress by preventing our failures of the past from stopping us, from inhibiting us. We must approach the present goal of today with confidence, with self-assurance that we can rise above failures, knowing we can hurdle the problem of living.

Remember always the old proverb:

Failure teaches success.

This Very Minute

It is appalling that, in these hectic and violent times, there are countless numbers of mental and psychoneurotic patients crowding our hospitals and institutions, and countless numbers waiting to be admitted. What is the reason? Tension! Too many of us suffer ills from tension by holding onto the burdens of yesterday and the fears of tomorrow. When we look in the mirror, what do we see? Sixty percent of what we see deals with yesterday. Twenty percent of what we see deals with tomorrow. But where is today? Lost in the panic of yesterday and tomorrow. Too many of us suffer from a disease that I call Yesterday Tomorrow Complex. There are 1,440 minutes to a day, and we live very few of them in the present. We must not live in the past any more than we should try to live in the future.

You must live today. Not just to exist or survive, but to live creatively, every day, searching for goals within your capabilities. You must realize that tomorrow is an extension of today. You must live in the present, every day, this very minute, live creatively, not destructively, live with belief, not unbelief. Here is what Pablo Casals, the great cellist, said when he reached his ninety-third birthday, "Every day I am reborn, every day is a new lifetime for' me." Live today, this very minute!

Success

Don't measure your success by counting prestige symbols and imitating other people, but by living the aspects of the Success Mechanism:

S: Sense of direction. You must have a goal, a goal within your capabilities.

U: Understanding. You must understand your needs and the needs of others. You may be an island within yourself, but you belong on the mainland with others. You must remember the words of Anatole France, "It is better to understand a little than to misunderstand a lot."

C: Courage. You must have courage to take your chances in life, to get your feet wet. If you make a mistake, try again. Try. Try. Try! Think of the words of Alfieri, "Often the test of courage is not to die but to live."

C: Compassion. You must have compassion for yourself as well as for others. You must see yourself and others with kind eyes if you want to be happy and discard the terrifying feeling of loneliness. Schopenhauer said, "Compassion is the basis of all morality."

E: Esteem. If you have no respect for yourself, no one will give it to you. Epictetus, a Greek philosopher, said, "What I made I lost; what I gave I have." When you contribute to life, you enlarge your sense of worth, your self-respect.

S: Self-Acceptance. You must accept yourself for what you are. Never try to be someone else. George Bernard Shaw said, "Better keep yourself clean and bright. You arc the window through which you see the world." We say, "Better keep your Self-Image clean and bright. It is the window through which you see the world."

S: Self-Confidence. You must remember the confidence of past successes in your present undertaking. You must concentrate on success like professional players in sports. They forget the times they lost in the past. They are out to win Now. You must use that technique to be a champion in the art of living, remembering that you cannot be a champion 100 percent of the time.

Look Inside The Husk

> *And what is a weed? A plant whose virtues have not been discovered.*
> —Ralph Waldo Emerson

When did these splendid words occur to Emerson? Perhaps one day when the harvest was ready to be gathered and the bright fields rippled in the wind with wheat for the winter's bread. For, ages ago, wheat was thought to be a weed, quite useless to mankind.

Perhaps on that day, looking at the ripe, bronze fields, Emerson thought of his friend and teacher Bronson Alcott, a tireless, undefeatable, unquenchable man. Perhaps he paused to reflect on Alcott's stubborn insistence that it was never the "bad boy" or the dullard who was erring, but those who lacked patience to probe beneath the surface, however unpromising or unfriendly, to discover what was there. There were no "weeds" in Bronson Alcott's schoolroom.

So many times, in clinics and in hospital wards, I have seen the apparently hopeless misfit transformed into a hopeful and helpful person—into a giver, not a taker—by the simplest display of interest and belief in him. It makes me wonder how many good citizens, creators and builders, contributors to our health as a nation, have been lost because someone, somewhere, was misled by the husk and did not see the golden grain within.

I suppose it comes down to this: our first must for every day should be to pause before passing judgment, remembering that the apparently useless weed may, with care and cultivation, provide tomorrow's bread.

On Selfishness

William Gladstone said, "Selfishness is the greatest curse of the human race." It is evil and immoral in that it prevents the person afflicted with this dread disease from growing into maturity. He does not set worthwhile goals and keeps others from reaching theirs. It is painful that selfishness finally adds up to unhappiness and loneliness. Selfishness is cancerous. It robs you of emotional and spiritual security, leaving you an empty human being. If you are a taker and live only for yourself, you wind up by yourself, and what kind of *self is* that when you cannot communicate with yourself or with others in a creative way.

It is natural in life to look for security by taking from life through some useful goal where you do not step on other people's toes and where you do not step on your own toes. If you receive, learn to give in return to others who are in desperate need of good will and compassion. The cure for selfishness is setting goals, creative goals for others and for yourself, for people, ideas, and for causes. The person with only self-interest is nearly always doomed, since self-interest makes him less than what he really can be and leads to atrophy of the mind, spirit, and body. If your self is used for you alone, you stay alone. If your self is used to understand your needs and the needs of others, you have friends. Which shall it be, selfishness or self-fulfillment? Remember the words of Sir William Osler, "We are here not to get all we can out of life for ourselves, but to try to make the lives of others happier."

On Humor

Mencius said, "The great man is he who does not lose his child's heart." And a child's heart is full o' humor, full of laughter—the child on a swing, the child on a pony, the child making sand worlds or the beach, the child dancing, the child running with cheerful playmates. The world of children is a serious world, but it is also a world characterized by laughter and joy.

We are more apt to display a sense of humor when we are ourselves. We become devoid of humor when we are pompous, pretentious, obviously hiding an unmistakable feeling of inferiority. We cannot enjoy a true sense of humor when we feel inferior. What is the value of humor anyway? It is an important value, since this trait belongs to the family of well-being, to the family of wholesomeness, and to the art of relaxation so desperately needed in our times. Humor is there for the asking for anyone who refuses to take himself too seriously, who is willing to let go of tensions even for a moment, to laugh and break the circuit of distress to which we are all heir. Of course, laughter should never be an unkind corrective or a form of ridicule. That's not laughter, that is envy or revenge. Then it is not relaxation, but an invitation to tension.

If you say you have never had a sense of humor, I don't believe you. You merely didn't permit humor to grow in your life. Here is a little exercise to practice if you are frowning. Go to the mirror and try to frown with your mouth wide open. You'll suddenly find yourself laughing, and the greatest expression of humor is laughing at yourself before you laugh at others.

On Making Mistakes

One of the tragedies in life for many of us is that we want to be perfect. We dread making a mistake, and when we do, we reprimand ourselves, can't live with ourselves. We're full of tension, unable to concentrate, unable to sleep, unable to find peace of mind. For that reason, the fear of making a mistake is the worst mistake of all, because it creates fear, uncertainty, inferiority. It makes our image shrink to the size of a small potato without ever testing true worth. After all, a mistake can be corrected, so why must we suffer endless torture? Why must we give away hope and belief in ourselves before we try to find out who we are and what our potential may be? And very often, mind, spirit, and body suffer enormously through an error, a blunder, a mistake.

The greatness in man consists of trying to be great, and you cannot be great if you demand of yourself to be faultless. Such a ridiculous demand results in isolation and emptiness. The true greatness in any human being lies not so much in making a mistake as in rising above it. We are all mistake makers, but thank God we have the power to be mistake breakers. The capacity to rise above a mistake is the beginning of success in the three worlds in which we live, in the body, in the mind, and in the spirit.

Thank God for a mistake, a blunder, a misfortune, an error. They give us an opportunity to make something of ourselves, to find our true worth, our big self. That is what success is all about. Remember the Words of Wang Yang-Ming, a Chinese philosopher, "The sages do not consider that making no mistakes is a blessing; they believe, rather, that the great virtue of man lies in his ability to correct his mistakes and continually to make a new man of himself."

Winning

I'd like to tell you about a memorable Kentucky Derby. Over 100,000 spectators stood and sang in the rain as the band played "My Old Kentucky Home."

Excitement mounted as the horses reached the starting gate, and the crowd tensed as the starter shouted, "They're off!" The Kentucky Derby is an exceptionally exciting event; and for the countless thousands who watch the Derby on TV or hear it reported on radio, it is in a class by itself.

The contest, a grueling test, was over quickly in two minutes—and to the jockey who won the "Run for the Roses" it was a marvelous prize.

Yes, two minutes and it is over, and one man becomes a champion. Can you be a winner, a champion in your own Derby? I believe you can; I believe all of us can.

Our "Kentucky Derby" is a special kind that we can win every day of our lives. How? Every day we allot two minutes to ourselves. We sit in a quiet room, and we become a racing contender. We see ourselves running for our self-respect. We imagine we are running toward our goal—without holding ourselves back with negative feelings. Every day is a new day, a new lifetime for us, when we can become winners and can use the confidence of past successes in our present undertaking. When we do this, when we keep our mind on our self-respect, we never lose. We are always the winner in the run for self-fulfillment, the greatest "Run for the Roses" of mankind.

And do you know something? When you run your own Kentucky Derby, it is always sunny. You can always find the sun within yourself if you will only search.

Bluffing

Does bluffing help achieve success? No. Absolutely not. In the end, you wind up fooling yourself. Shakespeare said, "To thine own self be true." What he said long ago is valid today, even though we live in frantic times in which too many people are takers in life, caring little for others. This can never lead to happiness or tranquility. I know millionaires who are just as miserable in the south of France as they are in New York or Dallas or Los Angeles, simply because they were merely takers and never thought of giving **to** others.

Bluffing is pretense; and when you pretend, you play games with yourself and with others, false games that leave you empty as a human being and lead to despair and self-destruction. You are part of life and a part of others. You belong to others whether you like it or not, and you can't live creatively and successfully if you fool others and fool yourself. pretend**ing** uses up too much valuable energy on a negative, worthless purpose.

We all wear colored glasses when it is sunny to protect our eyes. You must not wear symbolic glasses to color your entire life, to make believe what you are not. If you do, you put yourself behind the eight ball. It never works. See things as they are; live life as it is. See yourself with kindly eyes, and you will suddenly become important. Rise above your errors with truth. Help others. You can, and it will bring you a great feeling of satisfaction to share your happiness with others.

Daily Requirements

What are the daily requirements of man? There are many, but the following are the most important. I call these the daily dozen.

1. **Love.** Without it, we cannot survive. This incorporates love between man and woman and the psychological and spiritual love of mankind, which is the foundation upon which we build the Brotherhood of Man.

2. **Security.** There is a need for financial security, but there is also a very great need for emotional and spiritual security within oneself that will provide peace of mind.

3. **Self-expression**. We need to do something creative in this world instead of being just idle bystanders.

4. **Recognition.** We must feel acceptance by others, but first, we must find acceptance within ourselves and recognize our own worth.

5. **New creative experiences.** These determine our growth and maturity. We must continually remain alert for new opportunities to express ourselves creatively.

6. **Self-respect.** More than anything else, we should value self-respect and the respect of others and for others.

7. **Getting more living out of life.** Instead of being passive vegetables, we must create a richer life, each on his own terms, by his own standards.

8. **Sharing happiness with others.** Man should value his capacity to give. Young people must be taught this value. It is one of the most valuable assets in a happy life.

9. **Involvement.** One of the essential requirements for people of all ages.

Seek to help others who need your courage, your understanding, your good will

10. **The art of relaxation.** We need to get rid of our tensions and recharge our creative energies for peace.

11. **Reaching goals.** It is through reaching daily goals that we reach personal success and maturity.

12. **Rising above a mistake.** We must learn to see the errors in daily life, and we must learn to forgive ourselves so that we can approach new goals with clarity of mind and conscience.

The Real You

Finding the real you is not a job that takes a moment, or a day, or a month, or a year. It's a job of a lifetime; and finding the real you should be a great, joyous adventure in self-fulfillment. How can you find the real you? You must remember that the real you is composed of many assets and many liabilities. When you look in the mirror, you see a composite of assets: self-respect, confidence, self acceptance, and courage. These are your liabilities: frustration, loneliness, resentment, and inferiority feelings. Now the business of finding the real you lies in knowing what the liabilities do to your self-image. They create your little self. The positive aspects, your assets, create your big self. You are a combination of the big-self mechanism, which works to make you grow tall, and the little-self mechanism, which can make you become small. The negative feelings of the little-self mechanism are usually there. They are like warning lights. They tell you to take stock of your assets and do something with them. Your big-self mechanism is your green light, telling you to go forward, to reach goals within your capabilities, and to refuse to let your negative feelings shrink you to the size of a microbe.

How can you find the real you? By realizing that you can never reach total perfection; but you can get a tremendous amount of joy out of life by doing your best every day. And what is doing your best? Finding the real you by rising above personal problems, by rising above daily difficulties, rising above agitation, frustration, and feelings of loneliness and emptiness. As long as you think in creative terms, as long as you try to achieve goals in the present within your capabilities, you are on the road to finding the real you. Every day is a new day, a new opportunity; and as long as you persist in finding yourself, you will achieve fulfillment and be able to express the godlike quality within you.

Our World

Where do we belong? First of all, we belong to ourselves. We are an island within ourselves. That island can be as barren as rocks on the moon or as fruitful as an orchard or a beautiful countryside. It is within us to make of ourselves what we want to be—creatively, not destructively. You train for your goals, but they must be realistic, not dreams beyond your reach.

Man is a beautiful island within himself. During moments of stress and tension, he can take a vacation. He can take this vacation every day for a few moments, and its costs him nothing. The daily vacation is within you, in the room of your mind. For five minutes or so, you should vacation every day, making a habit of it like brushing your teeth, until it becomes second nature with you. Go on this vacation when pressures are great. Relax for a few minutes, let go of the tensions, renew your energies for the problems before you.

Yes, it is wonderful to be an island within yourself briefly, but you must not stay that way. You belong to yourself, but you also belong to the world. Happiness lies within the world, not totally within yourself. Prepare yourself to be a big self, but realize that the big self belongs to other people, too, who need your help. Man reaches his true big self when he shares his success and his big self with others. He shares his courage with' others when times are tough when there is pressure. He stands up for himself and for others, turning a crisis into an opportunity. The world is always full of crises, and we are here to help each other rise above them, to reach fulfillment and, sooner or later, the Brotherhood of Man.

Being Somebody

The first thing to remember is that no person—absolutely no one—has final authority over your destiny but you. You may honor or respect a parent or a close friend, but the closest friend you will ever have is yourself. You must be a friend to yourself first. You must respect yourself first, you must be a success with Yourself before you can be a success with others. The greatest treasure you will ever have is Your self-image, a good opinion of yourself, and You must never let anyone take this away from you, no matter who it may be. If anyone does, he is opinionated and wants you to live his life, not your own.

Of course, you might listen to words of advice from a parent or friend; but in the final analysis, you must make the decision of what you want to be, if 'what you want to be is within your capabilities and your training, if what you want to be doesn't mean stepping on other people's toes. Go toward your goals aggressively, refusing to let anyone steer you from your course, because you must believe in your goals, and you must drive to reach them.

Your goals, your parents' goals, your friends' goals are different. You must do the thing you feel you have to do; and you must apply the power. It is another way of saying that you must let your belief in yourself work for you, not against you. You must choose your career because you believe in it. Never choose a career to suit someone else. It is the beginning of failure and unhappiness. Respect the integrity of others, but respect your own integrity as well. You are the master of your own destiny.

Beauty

Ponce de Leon once searched for the Fountain of Youth and Beauty in Florida. But you will never find true beauty anywhere in the world as easily as you will find it in your own backyard; or, more specifically, inside yourself.

If you are resentful, full of hatred, envy, jealousy, and conceit, chances are you will look ugly to others and to yourself even if you are physically attractive. External beauty is important, and we should try to be physically attractive as long as possible. Still, young people must learn to realize that inner beauty is far more important than external beauty, because we get older whether we like it or not, but inner beauty can stay with us even at an advanced age.

What is inner beauty? Sharing your happiness and good fortune with others; accepting yourself for what you are, not trying to be someone else; forgiving others and yourself for errors that happened yesterday; seeing the good in yourself and in others and adjusting yourself to realities; longing for the better you inside yourself and inside others and searching every day for self-respect and the respect of others. These are qualities that will give you everlasting inner beauty, that will make you feel more beautiful and look more beautiful. This is the kind of beauty anyone can achieve at any age, even if they don't come up to the rigorous standards of classical beauty advertised on TV. Wouldn't it be just wonderful if inner beauty were emphasized on TV?

Bigotry

A bigot is a person who holds blindly to his own creeds and opinions and finds no room in his heart or mind for anyone else's. The word "bigotry" comes from the Spanish expression "man with a mustaches." However, in modern usage, it implies a hostile and biased attitude. People who practice bigotry don't realize that it means inner hostility and the destruction of one's self.

What is the anatomy of bigotry? It consists of the following: *Belligerent.* You are belligerent to yourself before you can be belligerent to others. *Intolerant* You're intolerant of yourself before you can be intolerant of others. *Grotesque.* You appear grotesque to yourself before you appear that way to other *Opinionated.* Your opinion counts—no one else's—and you thrust your viewpoint on others. Terror. You terrorize yourself, and you foist your terror on others' *Revenge.* There is a feeling of self-destruction within you, and you want to destroy others. The "Y" in bigotry is *You. You* are irrational with yourself, so you are irrational with others. You lacerate yourself, so you want to lacerate others. You're uncooperative with yourself, and you are uncooperative with others You endure the torture of tension, and you live to create tensions for others. You have gout of the mind, and you want to inflict your agony on others. You resent yourself, and you get false pleasure resenting others. You have eliminated yourself from happiness, so you curse others.

Bigotry is self-inflicted intolerance of self, leading to the wounding of others. Bigotry is self-denial. Only when you realize how terrible and destructive bigotry is to you will you, for your own peace of mind, turn your back on this evil force.

Faith and Belief

Often at the beginning of my career as a public speaker, I would be overcome with the panic of doubt, a lack of belief in myself, just before I got to the platform to deliver my talk. How would I begin? What would I say? What mistakes would I make? How could I stand there for an hour and face hundreds of people? How could I get through? But when the time came, I was there. I carried on because I had something to say. I did the best I could, and I came through with flying colors. And I learned that many of our best actors and actresses are especially nervous just before the curtain goes up.

All of us have self-doubts at the beginning of some under-takings whether we are doctors, lawyers, engineers, teachers, students, poets, or salesmen.

Where does faith and belief come from? From within ourselves. We are faith. We are belief. We are also doubt and unbelief. We as individuals must make the decision where we want to go in life, to be the big self or the little self. We must think of our faith and our belief as wings that can make us soar to our destination, to achieve our goals and reach self-fulfillment no matter how critical our times may be.

With doubt and unbelief our creative wings are clipped for the moment, and we can't get off the ground to rise above our self-imposed dungeon. We must thank God for doubt and unbelief. It is our moral responsibility to rise above them to make something of ourselves through faith and belief. These characteristics are eternally within us, waiting to be recognized, waiting for action.

Remember the words of William Blake:

> *If the sun and moon should doubt,*
> *They'd immediately go out.*

On Knowledge

Aristotle said, "All men desire by nature to know." He wrote this over two thousand years ago, but it is still true today. Of course, when he said, "all men," he meant everybody: men and women, rich and poor, black and white, young and old. I suppose there are about ten percent of people who never want to learn, ten percent who know it all; but look at the potentiality of the Brotherhood of Man when eighty percent of all people want to learn to improve, to get more living out of life, and to share this good fortune with others.

Man lives in three worlds: the body, the mind, and the spirit. If he stops eating, something happens to him physically. If he stops wanting to learn, something happens to him mentally and spiritually. No food, anemia of the body. No learning, anemia of the mind and spirit. In neither instance can you move in the world creatively and amount to your big self, because you will be working under severe handicaps.

Aristotle tells us what we already know, that every American—every human being—needs, deserves, and should have education. It is as natural for people to learn as it is for them to breathe. Learning is their nucleus of growth and accomplishment. It is also well to remember that the greatest adventure in learning is in getting to know yourself better, and that envy, hatred, stubbornness, indecision, indolence, and fear prevent such an experience. We must resolve to educate our minds to search for and find our big self.

On Vanity

Thomas a' Kempis said, "He is truly great that is little in himself and that maketh no account of any height of honor." These words are the quintessence of humility, when one is not arrogant of his successes, nor does he complain about his misfortunes. He insists on living creatively every day, every minute, to give happiness to himself and to share it with others. The reverse of this characteristic is vanity, a common trait that infects the mind and spirit of humanity. It's a matter of fact; no one can escape it entirely in a lifetime.

When you have vanity, you have conceit; and in both instances you falsely believe you are more than what you are when, as a matter of fact, you know the truth—that you are less, much less, than what you can be. Then, in your secret embarrassment, you scratch for attention, but it leads to naught. It's like scratching on marble. If the truth be known, you wind up disliking yourself, lost to yourself, neglecting opportunities to find your big self and worthwhile goals. There is nothing in vanity but defeat. Perhaps you would think twice before being vain if you realized that you are playing a depression game, a losing game that automatically makes you a member of the opinionated club; that you become a little dictator who cannot win, who cannot relax, who cannot sleep.

The cure: Think kindly of yourself, but don't gloat over successes. Be a good friend to yourself and you will be a good friend to others. Like Thomas Kempis said, you will be truly great if you don't make too great an account of your honors.

Being Yourself

Most people who have failed in an undertaking don't like what they see when they look in the mirror. Young people particularly are affected by this kind of emotional reaction to a problem that seems to defy solution. Just remember that as long as you live, you'll be making mistakes now and then; and when you do, it is only natural for you not to like yourself, not to like the image you see of yourself in the mirror, not to like your little self. The point to remember in being yourself is that you must rise above your little self. You must rise above mistakes and misfortunes of yesterday. You must try to reach your big self.

People are mistake makers, but they are also mistake breakers. The business of being yourself—your big self—is to accept yourself for what you are when you make mistakes. Look at yourself in the mirror with kind eyes and realize that you are much bigger than any error, any blunder, any misfortune, any heartache. You must live beyond your mistakes instead of with them. You must accept your weaknesses, stand on your feet in moments of crisis, and rely on the confidence from past successes to turn crises into creative opportunities.

If you don't like what you are, get off your own back. Stop living with this hang-up, because you and you alone can either like or dislike what you are. Realize now that you can be your better self, your big self, by rising above your mistakes. That's what successful living is all about. That's what being yourself is all about.

Embarking on a New Career

A new career? You're not even entrenched in your selected career, you say? But this is a different kind of career. It doesn't just make you money; it makes one a fuller human being.

That is your goal as you embark on your new career: to make yourself a fuller human being, to make yourself a more professional human being. Your goal is victory for you. You will climb Mount Everest.

Resharpen your focus. What if you can't remember X's batting average, or Y's RBI'S, or Z's earned-run average or won-lost record. So what?

Resharpen your focus. If you wash your car only once or twice a week, it will survive. A few specks of dirt on your precious car, unwashed, unnoticed, unregistered, isn't life or death. So what!

You will find yourself with more time. You must create more time for yourself. You must bypass trivia so you will have time. What can you do with it?

Embark on your new career. Your goal: the evolution of you. Accepting your imperfections. Tolerating your weaknesses. Appreciating and developing your strengths.

How?

1. You must accept yourself for what you are and yearn to grow daily by moving away from negativism.

2. You must think and do creatively as you reach for productive goals within your capabilities and training.

3. You must learn to control the emotional riot within you that distorts and scars your self-image, leading to disaster.

4. You must give to yourself as a friend first, then offer friendship to others.

5. You must learn to love life now, not yesterday or tomorrow. Your real love is for today. You must embark on your new career TODAY!

Overcoming a Handicap

High upon a hill in a Central American country sits a house near a cliff, with the beautiful blue-green waters far below. A chair is on the lawn near the cliff, and now and then, a man of forty-five sits in it. This man is a baby specialist, and his chair is a special chair: a wheelchair. He cannot walk—he has no legs—they had to be amputated to save his life.

There was a time when the shock of this disaster almost drove him out of his mind. There was a time when he was tempted to wheel himself over the cliff; but that was more than a year ago. Today, you can see him early in the morning, with his artificial legs, seated in a car specially made for him to drive himself to the children's clinic. You can see him seated in his wheelchair in the clinic with his stethoscope as anxious parents come to him with their children. You can see him at work, bringing back health to bodies and smiles to faces. You can see contentment in his own face for work achieved every day.

He knows that though he has no legs, he is always running in the hearts of children and parents, running for them, winning a race for them as he once won races for himself.

All of us are somewhat handicapped. All of us are somewhat crippled in another sense. The frustrations of the day, the extra tensions of the day may be too much for us. And if I may stretch the metaphor, the legs of our mind are crippled, rendered useless through fear. We feel helpless. But we must learn to live with such handicaps. We must learn to rise above them. We must learn how we can get out of the wheelchair of fear, indecision, of hatred and resentment. We can throw away our crutch by overcoming emotional handicaps and by adjusting ourselves to the extra tensions of the day so that they won't cripple us, so that we can rise to our full stature of fulfillment.

To do so, we must not brood over misfortunes. We must direct our energies to some useful goal every day, including others like the doctor did.

We can all help ourselves when we help others. Remember the doctor sitting in his wheelchair, high upon a hill, smoking his cigar contentedly after a fulfilling day's work. The doctor rose above despair. We all must try to rise above despair and failure. This is what success is all about.

Remember the words of Virgil:

> *They can conquer who believe they can."*

Discipline

A hundred years ago in Vienna, countless pregnant women died in the General Hospital after giving birth. A Professor Klein said it was pollution from the atmosphere. A young doctor by the name of Phillip Semmelweis didn't believe it. Finally, he discovered that childbed fever was blood poisoning brought about by the contamination from the hands of medical students who examined the mothers. Professor Klein represented authority, the established order of things. Semmelweis represented freedom of thought.

Authority kicked Semmelweis out of the hospital, and for the rest of his days, he fought for his principles, fought for the truth, but authority wouldn't listen. Finally, Semmelweis examined a tissue specimen of a mother dead from childbed fever, cut his fingers accidentally, and soon developed fever and died. He contracted childbed fever even though he was a man, proving completely that freedom of thought finally triumphed over authority even in tragedy.

There always will be a battle between authority and freedom of thought. Its variation in the household is the authority of the parents versus freedom of expression by their children. Children have hope and the future on their side; adults have ' maturity and wisdom on theirs. But parental authority is wrong when it results in punishment brought on by a lack of open-mindedness and understanding. Discipline properly executed on the child, who secretly craves guidance, must have creative characteristics rather than the destructive trait exemplified in Dr. Klein's punishment of Dr. Semmelweis. Discipline is more a test of the adult who uses it than of the child who
receives it.

Understanding and self-respect are the guiding keys to creative discipline. These values will reach a child's heart, letting him know—that the effort is to guide creatively without rancor. Creative discipline creates a partnership between parent and child. It establishes meeting between the self-respect of the adult, who has already made mistakes, and the self-respect of the youngster, who will make mistakes. In creating this atmosphere of friendship and companionship, discipline reaches its goal, its objective. The adult is able to hold on to his self-respect, and so is the child. The important thing to remember is that discipline imposed on others can only be creative and effective if it reveals self-discipline first. We must control the emotions that make us fail—fear and anger—and use the emotions that make us successful—understanding and self-respect. You must not impose your self-image on your child. The child has its own self-image, and you must help the child realize that he can improve his self-image and be happy with it.

Remember the words of Seneca:

No one can rule except one that can be ruled.

Dehypnosis

Let me tell you of an experience my friend Alfred Adler, one of the great pupils of Sigmund Freud, had that illustrates how powerful belief can be upon behavior and ability. In my book *Psycho-Cybernetics*, I mentioned how Adler, as a boy, got off to a bad start in arithmetic because he couldn't answer a few questions. His teacher became convinced that he was poor in mathematics. One day, however, he saw how to work a problem the teacher had put on the board, which none of the other pupils could work. He announced as much to the teacher. She and the whole class laughed. Whereupon Adler became indignant, strode to the blackboard, and worked the problem, much to their amazement. In doing so, he realized he could understand arithmetic. He felt a new confidence in his ability to become a good math student. Adler had been hypnotized by a false belief about himself. Not figuratively, but literally; he was actually hypnotized.

If we have accepted an idea from ourselves, our teachers, parents, friends, advertisements, or from any other source, and if we are firmly convinced that the idea is true, it has the same power over us as the hypnotist's words have over the hypnotized subject. We are all hypnotized by our fears and frustrations because they become a vicious habit. They create a pattern we can't break, just as a hypnotized person can't break the pattern the hypnotist makes him follow. We carry negative feelings from our job to our home, to our bed, and then back to the job. We burden ourselves unnecessarily with extra tensions that make us less than what we are. These negative ideas have exactly the same effect upon our behavior as the negative ideas implanted into the mind of a hypnotized subject by a professional hypnotist.

The point is that we can dehypnotize ourselves from these extra tensions as Adler did. Regardless of how big a failure we think ourselves to be, there is the ability and the power within us to change in order to be happy and successful. This ability or power becomes available to us just as soon as we change our beliefs, just as soon as we can dehypnotize ourselves from the ideas of "I can't," "I'm not worthy," "I don't deserve it," or other self-limiting thoughts. As Bacon said, "Man prefers to believe what he prefers to be true." Think about it! Dehypnotize yourself from false beliefs!

Memories

In living, we all create memories, and we store these memories in a mental tape recorder. We can use these memories constructively or destructively. What should we do with memories? Keep them in proper perspective.

I remember on one occasion, I was asked to attend a reunion of my medical class. I couldn't accept at that particular time, but fortunately, twenty-five years after graduation, I attended a class reunion. I put on my tuxedo and went to the hotel to meet my colleagues, but I couldn't find them; I couldn't recognize them. When the guests finally seated themselves at their respective tables—those who graduated before me and those who graduated after me—I looked for my table—the Class of 1923—and there, I saw nine people seated around the table and one empty seat, mine.

I sat down, and the man to my right, a short, fat, bald-headed man, suddenly said to me, "Maltz, what happened to you? Your hair is gray; it used to be black!"

I looked at his bald head and remembered that he had had beautiful blond hair, and I said to myself, "I wonder what happened to him?" Both of us abused our memories.

We must learn to use—memories only to remember happy moments, so that we can utilize them for the present undertaking. In doing that successfully, we build memories—happy memories—for tomorrow. The misfortunes of yesterday must be forgotten, lost in the tomb of time. Every day is a new lifetime that must be lived to the full, creatively.

Remember the words of Macedonius (sixth century):

> *Memory and Oblivion, all hail!*
> *Memory for goodness, Oblivion for evil!*

Character

In my book, *New Faces, New Futures,* written many years ago, I mentioned this incident in the first chapter. Three men who believed they could judge character by facial appearance were gathered in my office: a playwright, a lawyer, and a doctor. They were looking at masks of patients made before surgery. The playwright said, "This person with a receding chin is a weakling."

"Wrong," I answered. "He's an aggressive stockbroker."

The lawyer said, "This man with the ugly gash on his cheek must be a gangster. It's a typical squealer's cut.

"No, I said. "He's a sedate businessman who was in an auto accident."

The doctor examined the cast with the broken nose and said, "This fellow looks as if he's been in a number of fights. Is he a pugilist or racketeer?"

"No," I answered. "He's a schoolteacher who fell on his nose when he was a child." I then showed them the casts of these patients after surgery. They were astounded. They could not believe that these normal faces had once been horribly distorted.

To this day, many people persist in believing that the face is an index to character. Many businessmen ascribe a good measure of their success to their supposed ability to read character from facial features. These are hasty, reckless judgments. Even Aristotle, that great Greek philosopher, made the same mistake when he said, "Noses with thick bulbous ends belong to persons who are swinish." We cannot say that a man has big ears because he is stupid any more than we can say that he is stupid because he has big ears.

As Professor Jastrow said, "Judging by behavior, expression, gesture, manner, conversation has far greater value than judging by looks."

I venture to say that the self-image is the only accurate guide to character., The self-image is the result of our successes and failures in life. Using past successes in the present gives us confidence and enhances our character. Being ashamed of our self-image because we are overcome by past failures in a current undertaking diminishes our usefulness, diminishes our character, and makes us less than what we really are and can be.

There is an old Latin proverb that says, "A man's character is the arbiter of his fortune."

The Tufted Puffin

There is a little island off the coast of British Columbia whose stony crags are inhabited by a species of bird called the "puffin." It is a small tufted bird, a tufted puffin. The most amazing characteristic of this bird is its habit of living in that spot only. Take it away from that area, and it cannot survive. It has no resistance. This tufted puffin is so fragile that it cannot endure or overcome stress. **It** dies if you take it away from its normal habitat.

What kind of bird are *you*? Are you a tufted puffin with sawdust stuffin'? Or are you a goal-striver, a stress-survivor? That is what success is all about rising above a problem, a stress.

There is a poem by Victor Hugo called "Wings":

> **Be like the bird that,**
> **Pausing in its flight awhile**
> **On boughs too light,**
> **Feels them give way,**
> **Yet sings!**
> **Knowing she hath wings.**

Do you have wings? Of course you have. Your wings are your faith and belief in yourself. And you can soar to your destination if you'll only give yourself a chance. Through frustration and despair, you tie your wings, and you cannot get off the ground.

What kind of bird are you? A tufted puffin? Or can you, with wings of faith and belief, reach your destination? I believe you can; you have to believe it too. You have to believe that you came into this world to succeed, to rise above fear, to rise above a stress, turning your life into a continuous creative opportunity.

The Cleft Palate

In my practice as a plastic surgeon, I have operated on many cleft palates. This is a hole in the upper lip. One out of every 2,500 children is born with this defect, which can be corrected soon after birth. After World War II, I taught surgeons in a number of Latin American countries how to perform cleft palate surgery.

In one country, a boy of seventeen came to the capital from a village in the interior. When he was about to be put under anesthesia, he shouted, "I'm going to die! I'm going to die!"

I assured him that I was his friend and that he would be all right.

He tried to be calm, but I saw terror in his eyes. Finally, the anesthetist put him to sleep, and I repaired the hole in his lip.

Two weeks later, the final dressing was removed, and I said to him, "Take a look at yourself in the mirror."

He hesitated. I urged him, "Don't be afraid."

That minute, before he slowly walked to the mirror, must have been a lifetime to him. Finally, he looked—and stared at himself in disbelief. I knew what was running through his mind. He saw someone he had never seen before. He turned his head in different directions as he kept looking at his new face. Finally, he turned to me with tears of joy in his eyes and cried, "I'm going to live! I'm going to live!"

Are you going to live? Have you an emotional cleft palate? Have you a cleft palate in your mind and soul because of some hang-up where there is a gap between you and your integrity, where there is a hole between you and your dignity? Many of us have. You must remove the gap. Be your own plastic surgeon and bridge the gap between you and your self-respect with threads of compassion and self-understanding.

Daily Pleasure

Do not set conditions for your pleasure.

Do not say, "I'll have fun when I make $10,000."

Or "My happiness will begin when I get on that plane for Paris and Rome and Vienna."

Or "When I'm sixty-five, and I retire, I'll just lie in a deck chair in the sunshine."

There should be no *ifs* about the pleasure in your life.

Every day, one basic goal must be an inner feeling that you deserve to enjoy yourself, whether you're a millionaire or a pauper. A millionaire with a weak self-image can say to himself, "Someone will steal my money, and then nobody will talk to me." A poor man with a strong self-image can say to himself, "While my creditors are chasing me around the block, I can enjoy the exercise."

Don't fool yourself; if you really want happiness in your life, you'll find it, but only if you can live with good fortune.

Let me repeat, if *you can live with good fortune.*

Believe me; I have known many people who could not live with happiness. After a great success, instead of relaxing, their anxieties would intensify. Everything and everyone seemed to be chasing the diseases, lawsuits, accidents, Internal Revenue, even relatives—in their minds. They could not relax until they once again tasted what they were really looking for—failure. Learn to court pleasure, not pain. Pay homage to its virtues; feel that you are worthy.

Find pleasure in little things: food that tastes delicious, friendship that is sincere, a sun that is warming, a smile that is meant to cheer.

In *Othello,* the sophisticated, worldly-wise William Shakespeare wrote, "Pleasure and action make the hours seem short." Short or long, make your hours ring and bubble with pleasure. Laugh at people who say that pleasure is not part of life, because they are ignorant; but forgive them, because they are not as wise as you.

Know that happiness is real, that it is internal, that no one can make you unhappy without your consent.

You must remember every day that happiness is a gift you give to yourself, not just during Christmas but all year round.

Humility

Recently, I was riding a jet on my way from New York to London, and I overheard a man and his wife talking in front of me. She said, "What a beautiful sight. How insignificant it makes us feel." He said, "You mean how grateful we are to be alive in this universe." This exchange made me realize what humility gives us. The purpose of humility is not to make us feel insignificant but in our own right to get to know who we are and to contribute to the universe. Great men like Einstein and Gandhi were humble. They certainly were not self-disparaging. They were self-confident about their knowledge, about their goals for humanity, their desires to make the world a better place for people.

Humility is not self-denial; it is self-affirmation, belief in our integrity and dignity as human beings. It is a blending of success and failure, where we keep failure in proper perspective in the past and success m proper perspective in the present. We let neither dominate us. It is the balance between trying to be no more than we are and no less than we are, not trying to be superior or inferior. It is poise, in that we do not inhibit ourselves by past failures, nor do we brag about present successes. It is an emotional thermostat that keeps us being ourselves, that keeps us young.

I remember many years ago I was visiting with an editor friend of mine and he noticed I was unhappy. A story of mine had been turned down by a magazine. He said, "Maxwell, what gave you the idea that you could be successful as a writer overnight? You'll get many rejection slips before you succeed." That editor taught me humility. I did succeed in time by overcoming errors instead of letting errors overcome me.

Humility has these eight ingredients:

1. Sincerity. Being sincere with ourselves and with others.

2. Understanding. Understanding our needs and the needs of others.

3. **Knowledge.** Learning that we are what we are and that we don't have to keep up with the Joneses.

4. Capacity. Extending our ability to listen and learn.

5. **Integrity.** Constantly building an inner sense of values and adhering to them.

6. **Contentment.** Building a state of peacefulness through understanding and not making mountains of molehills.

7. **Yearning**. Looking for new horizons, new goals, new successes and reaching out for them.

8. **Maturity**. The pot of gold at the end of the rainbow. With maturity you will understand humility, and with humility you will be a successful human being.

There is no humiliation in humility. It takes time to acquire humility, but it is worth it since it brings happiness. Or, as James S. Barrie said, "Life is a long lesson in humility."

Are You Creative?

Many of us are firmly convinced that people are born creative or noncreative, that only a limited number of people can create in different generations. Leonardo da Vinci, Shakespeare, Beethoven, Alexander Graham Bell, and Einstein all used their creative gifts wisely. Each one had the power to use his imagination properly, productively.

What are the characteristics of a creative mind? First, a sense of direction, a goal. Then, a problem, clearly defined, and all the possible solutions. After that, the selection of the best solution and acting on it. You must have the ability to forget a problem, temporarily, if it defies solution and the capacity to rise above failures.

I believe that all of us are creative. We have a creative mechanism working for us that steers us toward success. For example, the simple exercise of picking up a pencil. We forget that, as children, we picked it up clumsily, zigzagging in the direction of the pencil until we learned to do it successfully. This successful performance was registered in the mental tape recorder for future use. This, in a mild sense, is a creative effort.

We all can create because we all have imagination. We use it daily without realizing it. For example, when we worry, we use imagination in a negative way to create something that doesn't exist. We project on the screen of the mind scenes that haven't happened as yet because we fear we will fail. On the other hand, when we are happy, we use the imagination constructively. We picture a worthwhile achievement of the goal we seek by remembering past successes to achieve pleasure in the present.

We are all made up of failures and successes, and to think creatively, we must rise above the mistakes of the past and use the self-confidence from past successes in our present undertaking.

We can think creatively when:

1. We think clearly about a problem.

2. We think of all possible solutions.

3. We accept the best and act upon it.

4. We forget the problem, temporarily, if it defies solution. The servo-mechanism within us will do the job for us subconsciously by utilizing the ingredients of our past successes.

The greatest creative effort for all of us, great or small, is to create the habit of happiness. This we can all do by making a habit of it every day, by recalling the happiness of past successes and using this good feeling in our present undertaking. Remember Elbert Hubbard's words, "Happiness is a habit—cultivate it!"

On Being Opinionated

One of the great problems throughout the ages has been that too many of us try to force our opinions on others, implying that we cannot be wrong. This leaves little room for self-improvement and throws a roadblock in the path of success. Imagine ten of the greatest living painters seated at a round table painting an apple in the center of the table. Each will paint the apple differently because each sees the apple differently.

It is the same with opinion. Beliefs are different depending on many factors of birth and environment, and we color opinion by these factors. The tragedy of being opinionated is that it prevents growth, progress, and self-fulfillment. It implies perfection; and since no one can be perfect at all times, it is a foregone conclusion that the opinionated person—in defending his weakness—will be unhappy and isolated.

What can you do to prevent being opinionated? You can make it your business to listen, to hear the thoughts of others. You might be wrong in your opinion, and then you must have the capacity to make a worthwhile change.

Being opinionated is a negative trait; open-mindedness is a constructive trait. The first leads to failure and isolation, the second to success and friendship.

You can stop being opinionated by stretching out your hand of friendship to others, by learning from others, by reading that others have the same rights as you, that all of us came into this world to succeed and not to fail. You can thus reactivate the success mechanism within you instead of holding on to a failure trait.

Remember the words of James Russell Lowell;

The foolish and dead alone never change their opinion.

On Stubbornness

Life means change. Your image changes every day simply because you are different every day and the situations of each day are different; and that is the way it should be. Man progresses by change. Nature progresses by change—spring, summer, winter, fall. Can you imagine if a tree in the spring were stubborn and refused to bud and bear leaves, if a flower were stubborn and refused to bloom, if a vegetable or fruit were stubborn and refused to grow and ripen?

Are you stubborn? Do you refuse to change and grow in stature? Are you resistant to creative living, to a smile, to friendship, to forgiveness, to the Brotherhood of Man?

Michel de Montaigne said, "Obstinacy and heat of opinion are the surest proof of stupidity."

To get more living out of life, you must start getting rid of negative feelings that create stubbornness and obstinacy, envy, indolence; they all give rise to resistance that makes you shrink to the size of a microbe.

Are you a microbe or a whole human being? You have the answer within you if you overcome stubbornness through forgiveness and friendship to yourself.

There *is* one kind of stubbornness that is creative. If, after sharp analysis, you find your beliefs worthy of humanity, fight for these beliefs. That is not pigheadedness; that is constructive determination, growth for yourself and for others.

Patience

John Dewey, who was my teacher of philosophy when I was a freshman at Columbia University, said, "The most useful virtue is patience."

Patience gives us hope as we wait and wait for an end to the wrangling in the UN, when we wait for the dawn of a new world—one world, a people's world.

Life becomes more complex every day, and technocracy threatens to strip man of his individuality. But it is during this time of pressure that you can learn to relax. This is a time for creative concentration and clear thinking. Don't make haste or make waste, but sit in a quiet room in your mind and use your imagination creatively to relax, to control your fears, anxieties, and uncertainties, to find tranquility through patience.

Sit in the quiet room of your mind and use your imagination. You can see a motion picture of yourself on the screen—your assets and liabilities, your smiles and your frowns. And, since you are the writer of the script, the actor, the director, and the audience all in one, you can change the script. You can use your assets of self-respect and self-confidence to find the patience that is within you, ready to be utilized for a constructive effort. It is through this technique that you encounter fewer failures, fewer frustrations. You find the inner you, the better you, which is the beginning of patience because it implies forgiveness. Patience is almost synonymous with forgiveness, almost synonymous with peace of mind, *almost synonymous* with finding your big self.

Flowers

The other day, I overheard two men talking over drinks in the dining room of their club. One said, "Don't send me flowers when I'm dead. I can't smell them then." The other nodded glumly.

These two sentences tell us briefly that we in this world live by three essential emotions: love, hatred, and aspiration. One of our daily quests is love which, in itself, signifies that we strive desperately not to be alone. Hatred is more difficult to explain. We resort to it too frequently without considering that this emotion degrades us and robs us of our dignity. The third emotion is aspiration, a dream to rise to the very heights of our true self-image to achieve happiness.

We are always accepting a challenge to move forward, to turn the unknown of tomorrow into success and security. The man who said, "Don't send me flowers when I'm dead," is successful in every sense of the word. He has financial security, has two children who adore him, is compassionate toward the needs of others. He is a giver in life, not a taker. And he started as a poor boy. What he meant by his remark was that man gets along best in life by utilizing the worthwhile traits within him: belief, hope, self-respect, and self-acceptance. He said, in other words, that what we give we never lose and that we do not need bouquets from anyone if we live our lives creatively without stepping on other people's toes.

The man who listened has resorted to shady practices in order to be successful in business. In one stock transaction, he told friends to buy stock as he unloaded his own shares. This man has a lot of money, but he is not happy. He has few friends. He always says that money talks, and he buys his way in life. He knows little about relaxation or peace of mind. He knows he has enemies, and he pretends to thrive on it, but he needs pills to fall asleep.

Remember, we are our own plastic reconstructive surgeons. Every day we shape our future happiness or despair, depending on whether we understand or refuse to understand that we do not live alone. We must live in relationship to others; we cannot ignore the needs of others. When we cultivate self-respect and compassion, we automatically cultivate our own garden of flowers. We bring growth and beauty to our surroundings.

Remember the words of Dorothy Gurney:

> *One is nearer God's heart in a garden*
> *than anywhere else in the world.*

Your Untapped Wealth

It is a tragedy that throughout history, so few people have fully exploited their potentialities. Yes, almost all people have rich, untapped areas of talent.

Don't be a "doubting Thomas." Follow the example of another "Thomas," Thomas Jefferson, America's third president. Thomas Jefferson's accomplishments are almost beyond belief. His confidence in his powers must have been extraordinary. In the process of serving out two full terms in our nation's highest office, he negotiated the famed Louisiana Purchase, which some historians have called the outstanding bargain in American history. This was preceded, of course, by his famed drafting of our great Declaration of Independence.

Jefferson's other achievements as a statesman are too numerous to mention. Few American statesmen in our history have done so much; it is doubtful ff any have done more.

The astonishing quality about Jefferson was his full use of his creative powers in other fields as well. A married man with two daughters, he was the president of the American Philosophical Society, established the University of Virginia, and supported the first American scientific expeditions.' He was also a topflight architect, who designed not only his own home but those of friends.

I am not suggesting that you are in any way a failure if you cannot measure up to such monumental achievements as those of Thomas Jefferson. My message is simply that you should reach out to the world with your full capabilities, whatever they may be, that you should emulate Jefferson in utilizing your resources instead of blocking them.

Here are the words of William Hazlitt:

He who undervalues himself is justly undervalued by others.

On Giving Up

We all suffer from crises in our time—some of us more than others—but what is creative living but standing up to a crisis, turning a crisis into an opportunity to find your big self, succeeding despite a blunder, a mistake, a handicap. And when does the real action begin? When we stand up to despair and use our compassion and our self-respect, remembering we are greater than an error, a blunder, or a heartache. It is during a moment of crisis that we must call upon our own sense of worth, call upon our courage to use our mental and spiritual muscles to move into the world of people where we belong, not to be alone in a world of loneliness.

Edmund Burke said, "Never despair, but if you do, work on in despair." Burke knew, as all of us know, that despair does not comprise a day or even a week of unhappiness, but that it is one dreary day dragging on endlessly to another as if there were no hope in sight. And that is why he said, "work on in despair," because at a time of crisis, we can call upon our courage and compassion to move us into the world with others searching for the peace of mind we crave.

Each day is a new lifetime, and we cannot give up a day that has not come as yet; we cannot give up a new day without even trying to find the promise of peace that can come at the least expected moment.

Despair is a kind of suffering we all know. It means, for the moment, retiring from life; and we must not retire from life at any age as long as we live. Life will not allow us to give up. Which shall it be, giving up or giving the best that is in us in a crisis?

Relaxation

Every generation speaks about uncertain times. Born in uncertainty, living in uncertainty, we pass on in uncertainty. By living creatively, we bend uncertainty to our will so we can reach goals and a sense of fulfillment. We live successfully by rising above our tensions. We can do this effectively if we practice the art of mental and spiritual relaxation by remembering these four points:

1. Forgive others, with no sense of condemnation. A clean, clear slate—not forgiveness on the installment plan. I love you today but can't stand the sight of you tomorrow—that is not forgiveness. A difficult habit to learn, but worth fighting for.

2. Forgive yourself for *your* errors or blunders. Another difficult task, but you can do it. Forget the blunders of yesterday and make it a habit to live fully today. To err may be a human failing, but to forgive is a human achievement. Shakespeare said, "To forgive is divine." Still, who is asking you to be divine? Be human and achieve your fulfillment as a human being.

3. Keep up with yourself, not with someone else. Trying to imitate others merely forces you to play second fiddle. Remember, you can't be someone else without tension. Every day you must try to make your self-image grow; this you can do.

4. See yourself at your best. Stop concentrating on your worst. You are your most wicked enemy when you torture yourself with feelings of frustration every day. You are at your best when you practice confidence every day. You have a choice; select wisely. Remember, you must forget yesterday, and you can forget yesterday through substitution: thinking and working

toward your present goal. The more you think of reaching your present goal, the less time you will have for the worries and heartaches of yesterday.

On Faults

Thomas Kempis wrote, "How seldom we weigh our neighbor in the same balance with ourselves." I have spoken and lectured to groups of people all over the world for the past fifteen years, to people in industry, religion, and education. Now and then, I would ask those in the audience: "How many of you have expressed resentment at least once in the last thirty days?" And all the people in the audience would raise their hands, and there was always laughter.

Yet, with all that, it is a very strange thing indeed that our own offenses seem nothing compared to the offenses of others. When we have done something for which we are ashamed, something destructive that makes our image shrink to the size of a small potato, we have a scapegoat—we blame our conscience. We say, "My conscience bothers me." And then we quickly condone ourselves.

But when it comes to a fault, a blunder, a mistake, or resentment in someone else, how quickly we discredit the individual. How derisive we are at catching someone in a lie, forgetting the countless lies we ourselves have told. To grow in stature as human beings, we must remember that we all have faults, that we are a mixture of good and evil, success and failure, belief and despair, friendship and loneliness, fear and courage. Men are alike in that they can be their big selves or their little selves at various moments in their lives; and it is only through forgiveness that we can find our better selves a greater share of the time.

No Limitations

In the Bible, we are told that when a prophet was in the desert and hungry, God lowered a sheet from the heavens containing food. To the prophet, it didn't look much like good food. It was "unclean" and contained all sorts of "crawling things." God rebuked him, admonishing him not to call "unclean" that which God had offered.

Some doctors and scientists today turn up their noses at whatever smacks of faith or religion. Some religionists have the same attitude of suspicion and revulsion concerning anything "scientific." Everyone's real goal is for more life, more living. Whatever your definition of happiness may be, you will experience more happiness as you experience more life. More living means, among other things, more accomplishment or the attainment of worthwhile goals, more love experienced and given, more health and enjoyment, more happiness for yourself and others.

I believe that there is ONE LIFE, one ultimate source, but that this ONE LIFE has many channels of expression and manifests itself in many forms. If we are to "Get More Living Out of Life," we should not limit the channels through which life may come to us. We Must accept it whether it comes in the form of science, religion, psychology, or through other channels.

One of the most important channels is through other people. Let us not refuse the help, happiness, and joy that others may bring us, nor should we deny what we can give to them. Let us not be too proud to accept help from others, nor too callous to give it. Let us not say "unclean" just because the form of the gift may not agree with our prejudices or our ideas of self-importance.

Refuse to place limitations on your life.

Here are the words of Samuel Johnson:

The business of life is to go forward.

On Fair Play

The title of one of Charles Reade's novels is "Put Yourself in His Place."

You will be a happy human being if you make a habit of living with these five words until the practice becomes second nature to you. These five words, lived, not read, will put you on the road to maturity and self-fulfillment, because you will think twice before passing judgment on someone else who has a point of view different from yours and who wants to stand for his rights as you do for yours.

At a moment of stress when you are overcome with doubt and unbelief, when you are overcome with aggressiveness and fear, at that moment when you are ready to denounce someone, say to yourself, "What would I do if I were in his place?" Fight for your rights if you must, but don't fight for something wrong out of hatred or revenge.

Friendship is desperately needed in these chaotic times, and the first light and glow of friendship with others starts when, at a moment of irrationality, you ask yourself, "What would I do if I were in his place?

Most important, you must have a sense of fair play with yourself. Never denounce yourself because of an error; never become a displaced person because of it. At such a time, ask yourself as you look in the mirror, "Would I do this to my best friend?"

Desire

"Desire accomplished is sweet to the soul" (Old Testament, Proverbs XIII:19). Build an unquenchable desire for emotional control. To live creatively. To understand yourself. To master the inner destructive forces that could, out of control, lead to disaster.

No matter how great your positive forces, you cannot grow emotionally if your fears and resentments overwhelm you. Not even your enormous desire to live will always help you here.

How can you hold your negative feelings in check?

First, you must keep yourself alert. Your ears are supersensitive: when the alarm system inside you goes off, they hear.

Second, when the alarm goes off, you must refuse to panic. You must keep your fingers off the panic button, off the trigger. Instead, you delay action a while, you reason with yourself, you accept yourself.

Then you solve your crisis, whether it is internal or external. You work to snuff out the fire inside you, or to stop the burglarizing of yourself by yourself. You use your understanding of yourself, developed through your long efforts, to improve yourself, to regain your good feelings, your peace of body, mind, and spirit.

In defeating your internal negative forces, you keep alive your unquenchable desire to get the most out of life.

On Ups and Downs

The following words come from the sacred book of the Hindus, "Bear shame and glory with an equal peace and an ever-tranquil heart."

You are a combination of happiness and unhappiness, success and failure, joy and grief, compassion and resentment, belief and unbelief.

In other words, you are a combination of the creative forces within you that will make you ten feet tall and the destructive forces within you that will make you ten inches small. And creative living proves that every day counts. Every day is a complete lifetime that must be lived to the full. Can you live life to the full every day if disappointments make you walk away from yourself, make you walk into a dungeon of your own choosing?

Does a mistake, an error, or a blunder do that to you? Do these things make you a shadow, a ghost of yourself, losing your identity in a fog of uncertainty and despair?

The business of creative living is to keep calm in times of adversity, and doubly calm when good fortune smiles upon you. Of course, love and hate defy the rules of philosophy, but neither one should make you less than what you are. You are small if you succumb to hate, and you are just as small if you succumb to love of self. You stand on the foundation of your true worth if you are able to stand up under stress as well as success.

You Can Do The Impossible

Carlyle said, "Alas! The fearful unbelief is unbelief in yourself." Of all the traps and pitfalls in life, lack of self-esteem is the deadliest and hardest to overcome, for it is a pit designed and dug by our own hands, summed up in the phrase, "It's no use—I can't do it!" The penalty of succumbing to it is heavy both for the individual in terms of material rewards lost and for society in gains and progress unachieved.

As a doctor, I should also point out that defeatism has still another aspect, a curious one, which is seldom recognized. It is more than possible that the words of Carlyle represent a confession of the secret that lay behind his own craggy assertiveness, his thunderous temper and waspish voice, and his appalling domestic tyranny.

Carlyle, of course, was an extreme case. But isn't it on those days when we are most subject to the "fearful unbelief," when we most doubt ourselves and feel inadequate to our task—isn't it precisely then that we are most difficult to get along with? Aren't we taking out our feeling of inadequacy on our family, our friends, our fellow employees?

The reflection almost automatically follows that, rather than to make ourselves and everyone else miserable, it might be a good idea to take another look at the root of the trouble, the private Demon of Unbelief, who proclaims in his cold, sad voice, "No, no, it's impossible." It is that good hard second look —taken not just for one's own sake but everyone else's too—that very often reveals that the "impossible task is quite possible after all.

The Demon of Unbelief is the result of past failure, which inhibits us from being our true selves in our present undertaking. This distorts our self-image. We must leave past failures and the Demon of Unbelief in the past where they belong, remembering that we can reach our true stature of dignity only when we rise above failures and mistakes of the past. We must recall the successes of the past in an effort to reach s our present goal. This gives us the self-confidence, the self-respect we had in the past, and we can utilize these assets for the present undertaken. This will make us proud of our self-image instead of ashamed of it. In that way, what seems "impossible" is possible after all.

Remember the words of Edward Young, "What we ardently wish, we soon believe."

Do You Feel Superior?

The other day I watched a motion-picture producer on TV being interviewed about his latest picture, and it seemed to me he made a very poor impression. He was bored and talked down to people, revealing that he felt superior to the man who interviewed him and to the audience.

Was he actually superior? I'm sure he wasn't. He was con ascending, barely tolerant, arrogant, all of which indicated not superiority but inferiority, since these traits are distorted variations of hatred that demean people.

I recently attended a christening at a Franciscan church, and the priest—young, of Italian extraction, with a kind smile on his face—mentioned how poor and humble his little church was. Of course it wasn't said in any form of complaint, but indicated rather that he knew the blessings of humility.

One of our greatest gifts is humility, because only through this trait can we reach full maturity and be in God's image. By being humble, I don't mean weak and inadequate. I mean strong, but with ability to understand ourselves and others, to keep our successes in proper perspective in the present without feeling superior, without displaying condescension, superiority, or arrogance. People who look down on others think they are playing God, when actually they are playing the role of the devil.

The great tragedy of feeling superior is that it leaves no room for improvement, no room for making a mistake, which is the basis for improvement. Only with humility can we rise above failure and reach our goal of maturity and happiness. Only then do we really become superior, not over others but over ourselves, shoving that we have refused to deny ourselves the right to improve. Remember the words of William Hazlitt, "No really great man ever thought himself so."

What Do Your Hands Reveal?

There are no two people alike, no two faces, no two hands, no two fingerprints. Yet hands, like the face, reveal our emotions within. I don't mean that one can tell the character of people by reading their palms. At best, this is a pseudoscience, as inaccurate as telling the character of people by the bumps on their heads or the size of their nose, chin, or ears. What I do mean is that our hands can be the extension of our emotions, representing without what is going on within. A closed fist can indicate stress as an open hand reveals relaxation. Fingers also represent a language to the deaf-mute, to the men at work in the stock exchange, and to engineers signaling to each other as the steel framework of a skyscraper slowly rises into the air. Fingers also represent a symbol. The winner in a civic election will raise his right hand and separate the index and ring fingers to form a V for victory.

I remember when I was operating on patients in a hospital in Panama many years ago, I saw a boy of eight in the clinic who held his right hand in his pocket, ashamed of his condition. The index and middle fingers had been joined since birth, a not too uncommon condition. He watched some children who poked fun at him playing baseball, and he envied their good fortune. And when I asked him why he wanted his fingers corrected, he answered that he wanted to play baseball. It was his way of saying that he wanted to be part of youth, not alone.

A week after the operation, before leaving for Costa Rica for another clinic, I removed the final bandages from the boy's hand. As he looked at his fingers, I said, "Separate them." At first, he was afraid, and then slowly he did separate them into a V—something he could never do before—and said, "V for victory!"

And this brings me to my point. Fingers and hands can be of different sizes and shapes, but they all reveal the successful or unsuccessful part of our nature. Does our hand reveal the clenched fist of anger or the open hand of goodwill? The clenched hand of tension or the open hand of relaxation?

Does it reveal fear, resentment, emptiness, or does it reveal love, self-respect, self-confidence?

Let's keep our hand open as a symbol of friendship, offering to others the best that is in us. Let us, every day, for a moment, separate our fingers to make a V as a symbol of daily victory over failures. Remember the words of Montaigne, "Man is capable of all things."

The Minutes

How many minutes are there in an hour? As many as we want to put into it. We are responsible for the continual, unceasing flow of minutes that make the hour. That makes us what we are. When we have a goal every day, every minute counts. When we have no goal, when we are lazy, every minute flies away uselessly.

I know a doctor who wanted to be a plastic surgeon. He watched me do surgery one morning at 8 A.M., was fascinated, and wanted to be my pupil. I agreed to teach him. He came once, twice, and suddenly didn't appear. A few days later, he came to my office and explained that he had overslept. He asked if I operated in the afternoon. I told him that I always operate in the morning at the hospital because it is best for the patient psychologically. He never took the course. He couldn't get up early enough. He was lazy.

We are all made of assets and liabilities. When we have a goal, we make time. When we are indolent, when we procrastinate, we lose precious time with fear, unbelief, uncertainty, and loneliness, because these thieves take us away from creative living and happiness.

There are twenty-four hours or fourteen hundred and forty minutes in a day. When we have a goal each day, every hour means a day of adventure; we make every minute count. When we are lazy, we can't find enough time in an hour. It's like a day wasted. There are fourteen hundred and forty useful or useless minutes in a day. If we use these minutes to advantage, we are on the road to successful living and happiness.

Here are the words of Thomas Kempis, "Remember that lost time does not return."

Sleep

There are three eight-hour periods in a day. Eight hours for work, eight hours for diversion, and eight hours for sleep. These eight hours for sleep are nature's way of keeping the mind, body, and spirit in proper tone and condition, so that problems can be faced the following day.

Shakespeare said, "Sleep that knits up the ravell'd sleave of care." Yet sleep is one of our great concerns in these frenetic times. Fortunes have been made by pharmaceutical companies who manufacture pills that are supposed to induce sleep.

I remember a time after I had lectured on Psycho-Cybernetics and Creative Living at the First Church of Religious Science in San Francisco, I boarded a plane to New York. On the plane was a friend of mine, a producer of film. He took a sleeping pill, then asked me if I wanted one. I told him I never had occasion to use them because I fall asleep naturally. In the early morning, when we reached New York, my friend woke me up. He hadn't slept at all despite the pill. He told me he had been worrying about his next film.

We all have worries and problems; but I've learned not to let them intrude upon my eight hours set aside for sleep. By far, the greatest reasons for insomnia are tension, anxiety, or negative feelings that make us restless and prevent us from falling asleep.

Relaxation is the best preparation for sleep, because sleep is deep relaxation in itself. To relax is not easy these days, but we still can make a habit of it when, during the eight hours of diversion, we take five minutes off and walk into the room of our mind. Of course, this is an imaginary room. But since we live with our imagination every day, whether we realize it or not, we should take advantage of this imaginary room where we relax, look out the window, and see a geyser letting off steam. This is a symbol for us to release a geyser, to let go of tensions for the moment, to break the electric circuit of distress even for a second. Making a habit of this is making a habit of sleep. Whenever we think of troubles, we are not prepared for sleep. When we prepare ourselves for sleep, we must not let troubles interfere. Try my prescription. It may take time; but sooner or later, it will work, and you won't need a pill.

Remember the words of Publius Syrus, "He sleeps well who knows not that he sleeps ill."

How To Dig For Treasures

Archeologists, proud plunderers of time, have found hidden treasures in ancient Greece.

Digging near a vegetable-growing village on the east coast of Attica, Dr. John Papadimitriou, Director of Antiquities in Greece's Ministry of Education, uncovered fifteen wooden vases carved in geometrical designs, the first such find in history. Knowing that fresh air would decompose the wood, which had been preserved in fertile mud since the fifth and sixth centuries B.C., the archeologist rushed them twenty-three miles to Athens for a thorough preservation bath.

Professor John L. Casky, of the University of Cincinnati, found in Greece a Mycenean settlement dating back 3,500 years, complete with temple, palace, private homes with inside plumbing, and a municipal sewer system.

And so, from time to time, we hear of new excavations that bring old civilizations to light.

How useful it would be if, as creative archeologists, we dug a little inside ourselves. We don't need an axe or a shovel, or any instrument for that matter. All we need is five minutes when we are resting after a day's work. We should use these five minutes to concentrate on ourselves. Concentration is thought in action. A thought has a beginning, a middle, and an ending. We must reflect logically, one thing at a time, with a beginning, a middle, and an ending. Then we will come to the realization that we are not our mistakes or failures, that we have assets too, and that we must not allow our assets to be buried under Our Mistakes. If we understand ourselves a little better, we can remove the debris of failure, and we are certain to find treasures more important to us than those treasures from a bygone civilization.

Personal treasures are self-respect, understanding, self-confidence, and courage. We must discover these within ourselves to help us tackle life's problems, to help us reach our daily goal, to give us our true self-image, which, in turn, brings happiness. Here are the words of Appius Claudius,

"Every man is the architect of his own fortune."

Your Invisible Pill

Modern science has created experts in the manufacture of billions of pills. It is impossible to count the incredible number taken during the year.

I know an industrialist who travels constantly but never without a pillbox. Here is his daily intake of pills: a pill for indigestion, a pill containing all vitamins, a tranquilizer, a stimulant, and a pill to put him to sleep at night.

I believe people take more pills than they require, and I suppose it is merely an expression of the turbulent times in which we live. Besides medical pills, we take other pills during the day without realizing it; they are invisible and affect our emotions and peace of mind.

Some time ago, I was sitting in the restroom in a health club on the French Riviera, and I couldn't help but overhear two men talking. One said, "You know, Harry is a crooked manipulator. He takes sick organizations and makes them well after freezing out the original owner. Then he hides some of the cash in a vault. You know, one of these days, the government will get wise to him, and he'll find himself in jail. It's a terrible thing to rob a man of his business."

The other man nodded.

Actually, the first man, Sam, had taken an ugly pill without knowing it. He was spitting outvenom against another member of the club. If the truth were told, Harry would have been depicted as an honest man who merely was a little faster than Sam in making the deals. When we use hatred or revenge, we are merely swallowing an invisible pill that makes us ugly and repulsive. It takes us away from truth, away from ourselves into a maze of uselessness. We waste a lot of energy in the process, energy that ought to go toward constructive purposes to reach a worthwhile goal.

Hatred or revenge abuses most the one who uses it. How much better it is to use our courage, our self-respect, and our self-confidence to achieve a goal no matter how small—without stepping on other people's toes. If we make a habit of that, without realizing it, we use a happiness pill for our mental well-being instead of an ugly pill.

Did you have your ugly pill or your happiness pill today? Remember the words of Hosea Ballou, "Hatred is self-punishment."

Forgiveness

The "wrong"—particularly our own feeling of condemnation of wrong—must be seen as an undesirable thing rather than a desirable thing. Before a person can agree within himself to have his arm amputated, he must cease to see his arm as a desirable thing to be retained but as an undesirable, damaging, and threatening thing to be given up.

In facial surgery, there can be no partial, tentative, or halfway measures. The scar tissue is cut out completely and entirely. The wound is allowed to heal cleanly. Special care is taken to make certain the face will be restored in every particular, just as it was before injury.

Therapeutic forgiveness is not difficult. The only difficulty is to secure your own willingness to cast aside a feeling of condemnation—your willingness to cancel out the debt with no reservations.

We find it difficult to forgive only because we take comfort in a sense of condemnation. We get a perverse and morbid enjoyment out of nursing our wounds. As long as we condemn another, we can feel superior to him.

No one can deny that there is a perverse sense of satisfaction in feeling sorry for yourself.

In therapeutic forgiveness, we cancel out the debt of the other person, not because we have decided to be generous or to do him a favor, or because we are morally superior. We cancel the debt because we come to recognize that the debt itself is not valid. True forgiveness comes only when we are able to see, and instantly accept, that there is and was *nothing for us to forgive*. We should not have condemned or hated the other person in the first place. Therapeutic forgiveness is active forgiveness, turning your good thoughts into creative performance. Here are six points to remember:

1. Use foresight and clear thinking. Live in the present, but look toward your goal.

2. Seize opportunities to improve yourself now.

3. Develop insight into yourself to check negative feelings and rise above them.

4. Concentrate on compassion for yourself and for others.

5. Forget yesterday's trials; remember the good things.

6. Try to relax. You can if you live the principles mentioned in this book. If you see yourself at your best, not at your worst, and if you keep up with yourself, you will relax.

   Here are the words of Robert Browning:

   Good to forgive;
   Best to forget.

Receiving Gifts

Long ago, I was invited by the government of Nicaragua to operate on a number of people with facial disfigurements. When I got to the capital, Managua, I went to the Hospital of God and there examined the patients I had been asked to help. In the line were two children, a boy of eight and a girl of seven. They were sister and brother, and they were both born with a deformity of the upper lip known as a harelip. A rumor had spread that I would operate on just one harelip, and the boy tried to get in front of the girl. Then there was a scuffle. Immediately, I explained that I would operate on both children, whereupon the mother, who was the cook at the hospital, stood erect and sang "The Star-Spangled Banner" to show her appreciation. Then she rushed into the hospital.

Ten days later, while I waited at the airport, the father of these children—a huge man of about three hundred pounds—came to me with a little bag in his hand. He opened the bag, took out an old rusty pirate's pistol and an old stuffed lizard, and said, "These are my best possessions. I'd like you to take them as an expression of my gratitude for helping my children." I took them, and in the plane on the way to Tegucigalpa, the capital of Honduras, I felt happy that through my gift of surgery, those children became normal. The best gift in life is the gift of understanding. When the person receives it, he is happy, and his image is improved. The same thing happens **to** the person who offers it because, in that process, he too grows in stature, in human dignity.

Here are the words of Ralph Waldo Emerson, "The only gift is a portion of thyself."

What Did You Forget Today?

I know a man who hates his boss because he hasn't given him a raise. He comes home from his office resentful of the boss. And, unable to control his irritation now and then, he casts his resentment on his wife and daughter. Then he is miserable. He gets to bed and cannot sleep as he plans ways to do away with his boss. He gets up in the morning, deciding to tell his boss off; then, he sits at his desk and buries his resentment temporarily.

There comes a time when you get to bed and hit the pillow. You are utterly alone with your thoughts. And you take inventory of yourself, your assets and your liabilities. Then you ask yourself what you forgot to do during the day that has gone forever. Did you forget to smile at least once a day? Did you forget to compliment someone for a deed well done, for a word well spoken? Did you forget that you can be happy, that you can make a habit of happiness? Did you forget resentment, violence, these negative feelings that take you away from yourself and make you the small person you actually aren't? Did you forget that you were born to succeed in life? Did you forget you have assets within you that God gave you? Did you forget that you have dignity because you were made in God's image? Did you forget to be sincere? Did you forget to understand the needs of others? Did you forget to be compassionate? Did you forget to be self-confident? Did you forget to accept yourself for what you are and not try to be someone else? What did you forget today? Think of one thing you don't want to forget tomorrow. It will make you relax. Take stock of yourself. It will improve your self-image and give you peace of mind for tomorrow's goal.

Are You A Displaced Person?

During the time of the Nazi insanity in Germany and elsewhere, countless thousands of innocent victims were displaced in their effort to escape Nazi terror. Many found themselves in different countries of Latin America, even in the far-off reaches of the Orient. Many landed in various areas of Europe after the Allies conquered Germany.

I remember, many years ago, a middle-aged woman consulted me. She raised the long sleeve of her dress and asked me if plastic surgery could eradicate the tattoo on her arm. The numbers were: 138756. She had lost her husband and son in a concentration camp. Displaced to America, she met a man who fell in love with her and was going to marry her. She wanted the numbers removed, the past forgotten. She wanted to forget yesterday and start a new life today. I operated on her. She married the man, a machinist, and they now live in upstate New York.

Many of us who were never in Germany and who know little of concentration camps or displaced persons often become displaced persons without realizing it. Instead of being displaced by some outside force, we displace ourselves from our true selves when we give vent to negative feelings, emotions which throw us off balance and make us less than what we are. I mean the emotions of hate and violence, of envy, despair, and frustration. These destructive emotions make us walk away from life, from others, make us walk from ourselves into a concentration camp that we build with the branches of our minds, where we move in a circle of loneliness and emptiness.

It is well to remember then that making a habit of negative emotions destroys our self-respect. These disfiguring emotions are symbolically the tattoo numbers we ourselves place on our arms, isolating ourselves from reality.

We must resort to the courage and self-respect within us and use these qualities for the present to prevent ourselves from displacing ourselves from the goal we seek. We must not permit ourselves to be displaced persons if we are to live creatively. When we rise above failure, we move toward the goal of happiness. Remember the words of John Dryden:

> *Of all the tyrannies of humankind,*
> *the worst is that which persecutes the mind.*

Our Ears

Like fingerprints, no two pairs of ears are alike. Their remarkable variation in size, shape, and appearance is regarded as proof that they are shriveled organs inherited from some remote semi human ancestor to whom they were of more use. For instance, the dog and horse have pointed ears, as does the monkey. The human ear has two distinct peculiarities: the folded upper margin and the lobe.

Conceptions of beautiful ears differ greatly with time and geography. Lubbock wrote of the East Islanders who punctured and enlarged their ears until they hung down to the shoulders. To them, monstrously distorted ears were envied as beautiful. Our concept of beauty is different.

Disfigurements of the ear are many. One of the most dramatic ear tragedies of all time occurred in the life of Vincent van Gogh, the artist. Terrified, Paul Gauguin contacted Van Gogh's brother to tell him that Vincent, in a state of terrible excitement and high fever, had cut off a piece of his own ear and brought it as a gift to a woman in a brothel.

From the beginning of time, efforts have been made to find some relationship between the size and shape of the ear and man's mental and emotional capabilities; but there is no truth to such correlation, even though children with protruding ears are often ridiculed and nicknamed "jackass."

I remember years ago in Rio, Brazil, where I was operating on many patients who needed plastic surgery, a man of seventy consulted me about his protruding ears. I asked him why he wanted his ears made normal in appearance at his age. He said, "Doctor, ever since childhood when I worked on a farm in Sweden, I was teased by others with the word 'donkey.' I grew up, left the farm, came to Brazil, married a Brazilian woman, had two children, a boy and a girl. I became successful. Now my children are gone on their own. My wife is gone. But I can't forget the taunts of my youth. I never looked normal. I wondered if you could fix my ears now so that when I leave this world, God will see me with normal ears, the way they should be."

PS.: I did the operation.

The shape of the ear is less important than the sound it carries to the hearing organ within. And this leads me to the point. It is more important for us to learn to shut our ears to evil gossip and hatred and to open them to compassion and understanding. We are all children of God, and we are entitled to each other's respect. Remember the words of Epictetus, "Nature has given to men one tongue, but two ears, that we may hear from others twice as much as we speak."

Impersonation

"Impersonation" is a word with a negative effect. As used generally, "impersonation" implies that you are trying to be someone else—an athletic hero, a movie star, an idol. In that process, you devalue yourself, depreciate your worth, and fail as a human being.

What you must do—if you will allow me a little artistic license in my use of the word—is "impersonate" yourself Be yourself… whenever you can. If circumstances force you to adopt a protective facade, know what you are doing, and return to yourself as soon as you can.

Recently I was on a ship, the *Michelangelo*. We sailed across the Atlantic Ocean, from New York to Cannes, France. I noticed a stocky woman in her late forties. She was eating with some friends near my table, and she kept explaining to them how she stays thin by walking and walking and walking around the deck of the ship. She claimed that it took pounds off her.

But by the end of the voyage, she looked much heavier; her face was extremely full, and every time I looked at her, she was eating.

She was playing a game of make-believe, pretending that her walking lost weight for her while she gorged herself every meal and gained perhaps fifteen pounds during that short trip. It was a physical distortion, and an emotional one too. Most of us distort ourselves emotionally by pretending we are what we are not.

Accept yourself for what you are. This is your personal responsibility to yourself.

Remember the words of Miguel de Cervantes, "All affectation is bad."

"I Just Wanted To Help"

I recall a time I went to Lake Orion, near Detroit, Michigan, to talk to a group of priests who had succumbed to alcoholism. They came from all over the world and were treated for four months, then returned to their flocks cured. During the stage of sobriety, they used my book *Psycho-Cybernetics* as a bridge to walk back to themselves.

After lecturing, I went to sleep for a few hours. I was awakened at 1:45 A.M. Lake Orion is about forty-five miles from Detroit, and I had to catch the 4:35 lane back to New York so that I could operate on a child who had been seriously injured in an automobile accident.

The night man, after waking me, took me to the house of the priests' sanitarium and made me scrambled eggs and coffee. This simple action touched me because it was not his job, and I had not asked him to make a meal for me.

He stood there, bushy hair, rosy cheeks, and asked me if the eggs were okay.

"Fine," I said, and thanked him for putting himself out for me at 2:00 A.M.

"I just wanted to help," he said, and gave me a shy, friendly smile.

After some small talk, he told me about himself. He had a bad heart. Under his shirt, he wore a pacemaker, an electrical instrument attached to the chest wall. The instrument helped him keep his heart beating normally, enabled him to live and work as a night man at the sanitarium.

"Another cup of coffee?" he asked.

I nodded.

"I like to help," he said. "I really do. Since I had my heart trouble, especially, I live a good life. I like to help people, and I take other people's help. I've got no complaints."

On the plane from Detroit to New York, I thought about this man who lived a simple life and enjoyed it. I said to myself, "If a man who can't live without an electrical instrument will not give in, we can all learn the lesson that, despite our problems, we can stand up to the stresses of the day and refuse to withdraw from our strength. By activating our success mechanism, every day, we can live each day to the full."

Here is a quote from Pliny the Elder (23-79 A.D.), "For a man to help another is to be a god."

A Spiritual Face Lift

To live creatively, we must be willing to be somewhat vulnerable. We must be willing to be hurt a little, if necessary, in creative living. A lot of people need a thicker and tougher emotional skin than they have. But they need only a tough emotional hide, not a shell. To trust, to love, to open ourselves to emotional communication with other people is to run the risk of being hurt. If we are hurt once, we can do one of two things. We can build a thick protective shell, or scar tissue, to prevent being hurt again, or we can "turn the other cheek," remain vulnerable and go on living creatively.

An oyster is never "hurt." He has a thick shell that protects him from everything. He is isolated. An oyster is secure but not creative. He cannot "go after" what he wants; he must wait for it to come to him. An oyster knows none of the "hurts" of emotional communication with his environment, but neither can an oyster know the joys.

Try giving yourself a "Spiritual Face Lift." It is more than a play on words. It opens you up to more life, more vitality, the "stuff" that youth is made of. You'll feel younger. You'll actually look younger. Many times, I have seen a man or woman look five or ten years younger in appearance after removing old emotional scars. Look around you. Who are the youthful-looking people you know over the age of forty? The grumpy? Resentful? The pessimistic? The ones who are soured on the world? Or are they the cheerful, optimistic, good-natured people?

Carrying a grudge against someone or against life can bring on the old-age stoop just as much as carrying a heavy weight around on your shoulders would. People with emotional scars, grudges, and the like are living in the past, which is characteristic of old people. The youthful attitude and youthful spirit, which erases wrinkles from the soul and the face and puts a sparkle in the eye, looks to the future with expectation.

So, why not give yourself a face lift? Your do-it-yourself kit consists of relaxation and positive thinking to prevent scars, therapeutic forgiveness to remove old scars, providing yourself with a tough (but not a hard) epidermis instead of a shell of creative living, a willingness to be a little vulnerable, and a longing for the future instead of the past. Remember, your future happiness depends on living creatively today, every day.

Are You Easily Hurt?

Many people are "hurt" terribly by tiny pinpricks or what we call social "slights." I'm sure you know someone in your family, your office, your circle of friends who is so thin-skinned and "sensitive" that others must be continually on guard lest offense be taken at some innocent word or act.

It is a well-known psychological fact that people who become offended the easiest have the lowest self-esteem. They are "hurt" by things they conceive as threats to their ego or self-esteem. Fancied emotional thrusts that pass unnoticed by a person with wholesome self-esteem slice these people up terribly. Even real "digs" and "cuts" that inflict painful injury to the ego of the person with low self-esteem do not make a dent in the ego of the person who thinks well of himself. It is the person who feels undeserving, who doubts his own capabilities, and has a poor opinion of himself who becomes jealous at the drop of a hat. It is the person who secretly doubts his own worth and feels insecure within himself who sees threats to his ego where there are none, who exaggerates and overestimates the damage from real threats.

We all need a certain amount of emotional toughness and ego security to protect us from real and fancied ego threats. It wouldn't be comfortable for the physical body to be covered over completely with a hard shell like a turtle's. We would be denied the pleasure of all sensual feeling. But the human body does have a layer of outer skin for the purpose of protecting us from the invasion of bacteria, small bumps and bruises, and pinpricks. That skin is thick enough and tough enough to offer protection against small wounds, but not so thick or hard that it interferes with all feeling. Many people have no covering over their ego. They have only the thin, sensitive inner skin. They need to become thicker-skinned, emotionally tougher, so that they will simply ignore petty cuts and minor ego threats.

They need to build their self-esteem, get a better and more adequate self-image so that they will not feel threatened by every chance remark or innocent act. A big strong man does not feel threatened by a small danger; a little man does. In the same way, a healthy strong ego, with plenty of self-esteem, does not feel itself threatened by every innocent remark.

Poker Face

I know four women who meet every Friday night in one of their homes. For many years, this has been a ritual. They are quite unusual. When they get together, they don't smoke, they don't drink, they don't gossip. They are so fascinated with what they are doing, they don't talk about children, husbands, relatives, the weather, politics, or world affairs.

Sitting around the table, they conduct their business as if it were the only thing that mattered on Friday evening. Their business is cards: poker, dealer's choice. None of them plays it cagey; all are liberal players and sometimes reckless. Over the years, they have learned to know each other's game. Each has her special secret weapon, the knowledge of the others' facial expressions when they hold a winning hand. One coughs, the second smiles, the third frowns, the last tries to look astonished.

The game has been going on every Friday, year after year. Now it is at Harriet's house regularly because she has arthritis and has to sit in a special chair. They play, they enjoy themselves, and at the end of the year, they break even.

They play poker, but they do not wear poker faces. They know each other's game just as they know each other.

In life, people too often wear poker faces and watch other people doing the same; the idea is to fool each other. They corrugate the skin of their faces into all sorts of poses and affectations. This does not work. The trick is to do what these four women do every Friday night. The trick is not to trick. Be yourself. Be true to yourself. Like yourself and let others like what you really are. Don't be affected, don't wear a poker face. Just be natural and show that you like people, that you are willing to help. Let this true face be your poker face, and you will always have an ace in the hole. That way, you will never lose.

Confrontation

We hear a great deal of talk these days about "confrontation." What is the greatest confrontation of this generation? Is it the confrontation between young people and the "Establishment"?

Is it the confrontation between young people and the powers that be in education and religions?

Neither of these, well-advertised though they may be, is the greatest confrontation of today.

The greatest confrontation of today may not even show sufficiently to be observed by the people with whom we have everyday contact, because it takes place within each one of us; it is the confrontation inside us, and it involves the different sides of our nature. It involves our success and our failure instincts; it involves the meaning that we will or will not give to our lives.

Who will win in this eternal battle?

The abrasive side of you, hating every imperfection in yourself, afraid to take chances because you may fail or stumble, blaming yourself for everything you do wrong? Or the kind, accepting side of you, supporting yourself when you are weak or inadequate or unthinking or offensive?

The winner must be the live richly, and this is your come out a winner.

The Goal Of "Eternal" Youth

A human attitude, a compassionate attitude toward yourself, will be decisive in the success with which you are able to achieve your goals.

You must live with yourself and your image of yourself; there is no escape from this. You can travel to Paris or Calcutta, to London or Rome, to Buenos Aires or New Delhi—but you cannot escape. No matter where you are, you take yourself with you.

You are either your lifelong partner or your lifelong enemy.

A wonderful goal I hope you will achieve is the goal of feeling youthful always—regardless of your chronological age. I define youth as fresh, vigorous, alive; it is something that bubbles, that does not stagnate.

Champagne is youthful when it pours from the bottle, full of sparkle and zing. It has lost its youth when it sits untouched and unwanted; it is then inert, flat, dead.

Youth is song, it is enthusiasm, it is fire. It comes from the spirit, fills the mind, comingles with the success instincts, tingles in the bloodstream.

Here is a goal to pursue every day—if only for a few minutes—the goal of feeling youthful for as long as you live. Think of what you can do to make your days more fun. Use your sense of direction to point the way.

Remember your goal—more zest, more fun.

Youth—as long as you live.

Look for the youth in you. It will enrich your days and years of creative living.

This is one of the best goals of all.

Humanity—Toward Yourself

You must learn to accept your human weaknesses. This is of tremendous importance to you.

Most people, if they stop to think, understand the plight of underprivileged groups.

Most people, if they pause in the midst of a hectic day, are sympathetic to the problems of their neighbors.

Many people feel for the frailties and blunders of people they have never met.

And yet, these same people, confronted with their own human failings, are inhuman.

During the Spanish Inquisition of the fifteenth century, Torquemada earned historical infamy for his relentless cruelty. If you are familiar with this part of history, you likely feel revulsion on seeing his name in print. Yet you could be treating yourself with comparative cruelty.

When you stammer during a conversations' reflection of tension or confusion—do you forgive yourself?

When you burn the toast, and the three-minute eggs become thirteen-minute eggs, do you forgive yourself?

When you misplace a five-dollar bill or lose it,—do you forgive yourself?

When you forget an appointment, do you forgive yourself?

When your day goes wrong, and you lose your temper and shout and scream, do you forgive yourself?

You must learn to be human toward yourself, to forgive your shortcomings; otherwise, your success mechanism will not function, and you will not attain goals that will be really satisfying. Success and self-hate cannot live together. They are enemies, not partners.

When you rub the sleep out of your eyes and sit up in bed, tell yourself first thing, "Today, I will be human toward myself."

On Envy

In this day of prestige symbols, you are often more tempted to imitate others than to build your own self-respect. And when you imitate someone, you are playing second fiddle, and consequently, you can never find your true worth. You renounce your self-image and live in the self-image of someone else, and this means unhappiness.

It is the same with envy, a destructive trait that takes you away from yourself and prevents you from big self. Instead, you prefer to be becoming petty and small. You do not even imitate then. You are filled with wrath and lose your reason and sense of fair play. You think in destructive terms and seethe with resentment at another person's good fortune, hurting yourself in the process. The chances are that the person you envy doesn't know that you are alive. And alive you are not when you live in envy; you are merely existing, a small dark shadow of your true self.

Envy is high blood pressure of the mind that paralyzes you preventing you from becoming your
big self.

Is there a cure for envy? I think so. If you were to face the mirror to take stock of ourself, and realize that this trait is hurting you, you would think quickly about making a constructive change. How? By using compassion on yourself first, it is the beginning of wisdom and humility. It is the beginning of forgiving yourself for an error and rising above it. Perhaps you can start a new day for yourself by remembering the words of Ovid, "Envy, the meanest of vices, creeps on the ground like a serpent."

Your Worst Enemy

Many of us do not realize what we believe when we look in the mirror. Many of us do not see our own image but someone else's image that we feel we must please, thinking it might be of value. But there is no value or glory playing second fiddle to someone else. You cannot live your life with someone else's image. It means self-destruction; you become your worst enemy.

You are your worst enemy when you want to be perfect. You become fearful of making a mistake, so you don't assert yourself; therefore, you cannot achieve happiness in life. You cannot gain friendship that way or in any negative way where you symbolically walk around on your knees trying to get attention by trying to please everybody.

Friendship begins with you; you can't be a friend to others unless you are a friend to yourself. What is equally important is that you can't be a friend to everybody. We all see things differently. That is the way it should be; and because of that, it is inevitable that we will make enemies with people who violently disagree with us. If we firmly and honestly feel that our cause is right, we should not be afraid of making enemies but should try to maintain harmony.

There is an old Chinese proverb that says, "Just as tall trees are known by their shadows, so are good men known by their enemies." By far, you are your worst enemy either when through fear and indecision you live to please someone else, or when you refuse to live at all because you are fearful of making a mistake.

Negotiation With Yourself

You must negotiate with yourself. Insist on your human rights. You must try to narrow the gap between your big self and your little self. You must work to create a proper climate within yourself for the development of your total personality. You can do this by eliminating past grievances about yourself, by forgiving yourself, and by setting a limit to the inhumanity in yourself toward yourself.

The troubles in the Mideast and in Southeast Asia seem interminable. Don't let this happen to you. You must negotiate an end to the riot and violence within you, so that you can make yourself whole and healthy and move toward a spirit of brotherliness and full participation in living.

You have empathy for other people only when you have empathy for yourself first. Don't downgrade yourself, and then try to extend a helping hand to others. That's absurd! Empathy starts at home. It's a daily enterprise in a daily climate. You can pick up your telephone and dial the weather forecast. Then, daily, tune in to yourself to see how you feel, what you need. Does a mother, without really listening, hear her baby crying in another room? Yes, and you, without special effort, can listen for your emotional heartbeat, screening out the hectic hustle bustle of the world to give attention to your prime personal responsibility—yourself.

Sincerity

I remember a time when a mother brought two daughters to my office. The older girl was beautiful, the younger was ugly. She had a receding chin that needed correction. The older daughter suddenly said, "I don't see why she has to have any work done. God made her that way, and that's the way she should be."

Do you think this beautiful girl was religious? I don't. I think she was insincere. She wanted to be the only beautiful child in the family and resented the fact that something could be done for her younger sister.

On another occasion, I remember a humorist pretending he was a candidate running for election. He said, "Friends, I want you to vote for me for mayor for the simple reason that the symbiosis of the calcium makes it evident that I'm the right man. Besides, you must understand that the *resipse loquitor* of my dignity makes it imperative that I'm the man for the job." Now, these words and others that followed formed a lot of sentences that meant nothing—double talk. This, done seriously, is insincerity. Insincerity leads to exhaustion.

To be sincere, we must do three things: We must look behind us, within ourselves and, finally, in front of us. When we look behind us, we must remember the mistakes we made in the past in order to correct them and improve the future. When we look within ourselves, we must remember that we are made of assets as well as liabilities. We must try to enhance our assets as much as we can. Finally, we must have the capacity to look forward, to realize that the day—a full day—is a lifetime in itself and that we must have a goal for this day, a goal within our capabilities and training. When we reach this goal with integrity and with sincerity, we become useful not only to ourselves but to others. We are then on the road to happiness for the simple reason that we are improving our self-image, striving—always striving—for self-fulfillment.

Remember the words of Confucius, "Sincerity and truth are the basis of every virtue."

The Common Bond

Terence, who was born a slave and made something of himself in Rome twenty-one centuries ago, said this, "I am a man; nothing that concerns mankind is alien to me." He was a comedian and was the first to proclaim the principle of common kinship in man.

Whether he is black, red, brown, or white, whether his language is different from yours, whether he is rich or poor, whether he is a slave or free, whether his appearance is different from yours, whether his thoughts about life are different from yours, you have one common bond with any other person in the universe.

The suffering, the sorrows, the grief, the despair, the loneliness and emptiness, the insecurity and uncertainty, the doubt and fear are the same. We all suffer the same. But there is a far greater bond that can hold us together. The faith and hope, fortitude and persistency, smiles and laughter, understanding and courage, self-respect and self-acceptance, confidence and encouragement we can give each other in times of crises and in times of peace, seeking peace of mind. This is the greatest bond of all to hold us together as we struggle in the slow evolution from hatred, to tolerance, to love.

At no time in history has the call for unity of all people been greater than now. In this time of agonizing wars, in this time of the atom bomb that threatens man's very existence, I believe that human understanding and sympathy, I believe that human encouragement and dignity will hold us together for a better world.

On False Pride

Listen to the words of Carl Sandburg:
"Look out how you use proud words.
When you let proud words go, it is not easy to call them back.
They wear long boots, hard boots...
Look out how you use proud words."

Pride sometimes is a destructive trait—when it carries with it anger, prejudice, and resentment, when it knows nothing of compassion, love, or friendship. False pride means intolerance, arrogance, and ignorance—ignorance of the great fundamental truths of creative living, simplicity, humility, encouragement.

Man's great goal to improve and to make something of himself and of others less fortunate lies in his imagination, the power of his imagination to find his true worth. False pride means only that you use your imagination destructively to hurt others and, equally important, to hurt yourself without knowing it. False pride takes you away from reality, from the beauty of living, and you are then unable to find happiness for yourself.

The tragedy of false pride is that it is immoral and sinful in that it prevents a person from rising to his full stature of integrity. Can you have false pride and self-respect? Never! Can you have understanding and false pride at one time? Never! Can you have forgiveness and false pride at the same time? Never!

True pride comes from compassion for yourself—a happy combination of achievement and humility.

Proud words (undeserved) are not easy to call back. But you can call yourself back from the illness of false pride and find the big you through compassion for yourself.

Up Till Now

I had dinner one evening with a friend who is a successful businessman, married then divorced. He has two children, a boy and a girl, who are at college. After many years of living alone, he married again. I asked him, "Joe, how does it feel to be married again?"

He replied, "Okay, up till now."

"What do you mean?" I went on, "You've been married only six weeks."

He said, "Well, everything is fine. I don't have to run around, make all sorts of dates. I have a home now. I have companionship and peace of mind. I'm just hoping it stays that way. That's what I mean by 'Okay, up till now.'"

What Joe was thinking is exactly what most of us think, but in different circumstances. He was thinking about the future. We all live in hope for a happy future. This keeps us young, because the main characteristic of youth is hope for the future. The reason is that youth has no real past and looks to build a future as it moves toward the threshold of adult life. However, hope and the future are certainly not passive words. Passive words take us away from ourselves and lead us to nowhere. Thus, when we passively hope that when tomorrow comes, things will be all right, or when we dream of the happy past when we are failing in the present and hope that by some magic happiness will return tomorrow, we are not hoping for the future creatively. We are just using words, expecting the words to open the door to happiness when tomorrow comes. No one ever sees happiness when tomorrow comes; it is today.

To use the symbols of hope and tomorrow creatively, we must live for today. Every day must be a complete lifetime, and we must live it to the full. We must strive for a useful goal every reach it, even if we are momentarily sidetracked by failure. We cannot use the phrase "up till now"—it implies doubt, fear, and a lack of belief.

All of us must actively create in the new day when it comes. We must use courage and self-respect to keep love and companionship in true perspective. This is active hope, which builds a happy future by living the present day to the brim. This is the true hope for tomorrow that will keep us young. We should remember the words of Samuel Johnson, "Learn that the present hour alone is man's."

On Being Complacent

Being satisfied and pleased with oneself is one thing. Having respect for oneself is another.

If you have a goal and you reach your goal, it gives you confidence. You use this confidence to achieve new goals. That is what creative living is all about.

When you develop confidence on your own initiative, there is no shame in being proud of your achievement. You don't have to brag about it; but you can look at yourself with kind eyes and, with approval, you can accept yourself for what you are and what you can be. This does not mean complacency, being satisfied with your lot, and staying that way. Psycho-Cybernetics teaches that when you reach one goal, you start after another goal the very next day, never being fully satisfied with yourself or your achievements.

Complacency is a variation of conceit, because you like yourself and go on liking yourself for what you have achieved, feeling you need not achieve anymore.

Complacency and humility do not go together, but confidence and humility do. The danger in being complacent is that you become passive and rest on your laurels, whatever they may be. To become passive is to become inactive; and, when you become inactive, you retire from the realities of life.' Creative living means that you must always keep moving in the stream of things. You can still enjoy a vacation now and relax in the room of your mind to renew your energies and your courage to tackle life's problems. Complacency signals that you are resting too long. All rest and no work makes you dull, uninteresting, lifeless.

No one can make you complacent without your consent. If you are self-satisfied, it is a symptom of fear—fear of what is real.

Remember that complacency is God's gift to little men.

Our Impulses

Should we obey an impulse? We should if the impulse is constructive. Impulses can also be destructive. When we hate, we often, through imagination, dispose of the individual. This creates negative impulses that have no value because they distort the self-image.

We live every day with imagination. Worry is a form of imagination. Here we throw on the screen of the mind past failures, which inhibit us in our daily tasks of the present. When we are happy, we throw on the screen of the mind past successes, which give us the confidence we exercise in the daily tasks for the present. A good impulse is nothing more than imagination that seeks action to improve the self-image.

When I was a young man, I had the impulse, the desire, to be a plastic surgeon. This was during a time when the specialty was practically unknown. Despite tremendous objections from family, I
obeyed my impulse.

I know a doctor who, twenty years ago, had the impulse to be a baby specialist. He loved children and would have been excellent in this specialty. But he was undecided. He said he'd wait until he had saved enough money, until he could properly provide for his wife and child. One indecision followed another, and he never became a baby specialist.

Indecision is unbelief. Unbelief is fear. And this constant fear prolongs tension and, finally, puts us in a state of paralysis. This scars and distorts the self-image, making us less than what we are, preventing us from reaching our true stature of fulfillment.

I know a married woman who has two children. She suddenly had the impulse to do abstract painting. She followed her impulse despite objections from her family. Now she sells her paintings. She has made her family happy and herself happy. The point to remember is to obey your impulse, the good impulse. It is a challenge to be happy. It is a chance to put the imagination to work, to reach a worthwhile goal, to fulfill ourselves.

Remember the words of George Herbert, "He begins to die who quits his desires."

Ideas

What are ideas? They are the product of the imagination, of thinking and concentrating on a specific subject. An idea is a brainchild, but what kind of a child is it? Is it a child born of resentment or hatred? Is it a deformed child born out of deception and trickery? Or is it a beautiful child born out of love and encouragement, out of hope and belief? These latter children of the mind and spirit are so desperately needed in these chaotic times when it seems that a cannon **is** more important than a human life, that money is more important than goodwill, that the destructive thought of taking exceeds the creative thought of giving.

It is now, this very minute, that we have to search for self-respect, for the assurance that peace of mind can be ours in this lifetime. It is at this very moment, when reason and patience are undergoing an eclipse, when wars are intended to destroy the world forever, that we must live in the hope given us by creative ideas. We should strive to build ideas on compassion and humility, on love and friendship, on taking less and giving more while we are alive, if life on this planet is to be sustained for the future.

It is at this very moment that mass fulfillment demands that we see the good in others, not the evil; see the hope in others, not the frustration; see the joy in others, not the sorrow; see the faith in others, not the despair.

Great ideas are truths waiting to be fulfilled, and no idea is worth anything unless and until we turn it into a worthwhile performance for the benefit of all humanity.

Oliver Wendell Holmes said, "The ultimate good is better achieved by the free trade in ideas."

Grief and Loneliness

Grief brings loneliness. There is an ancient Greek saying that, of all ills common to all men, the greatest is grief. None of us can escape it. It makes some men tender and compassionate, and others—not as strong perhaps—it makes hard, encased in protective armor.

I remember after I graduated from medical school and became an intern, I put on my white uniform for the first time and was quite happy about it. I telephoned my father and told him about it. He was overjoyed and said he would take the subway and come up to the hospital in an hour or two to see me.

An hour passed and then another, and he didn't come. Later on, I received a telephone call. I rushed to another hospital downtown, and there, my father lay dead. He had been killed by an automobile.

I was overcome with grief, and I wondered if I would ever survive it. I couldn't get out of my mind the fact that my father was dead and that he would never see me as a doctor. Finally, I terminated my self-imposed isolation from others and returned to the world of people.

We can suffer up to a point. The body can endure so much torment; then no more. It is fitting; it is a need of the soul to grieve for a loved one lost; but the time comes when we must stop grieving and return to the joyful business of living. Endless grief becomes a self-destructive force that must be stopped, like a leak in a roof; otherwise, there will be a flood and enormous loss in its wake. Endless obsession over pain means separation from other people; it means loneliness.

Shakespeare believed that everyone could master grief, except the one who feels it; nevertheless, we must learn to master sorrow. Time will help us if we help time. The thing to remember is that we must eventually shake off grief and return to everyday realities—before the inner scar becomes permanent. When this happens, we have an illness—worse than an ulcer—which we contract deep inside ourselves, bathing in a form of selfishness that is unpleasant and leads to a feeling of loneliness. Then one may find false pleasure indulging in grief, proving Samuel Johnson's contention that grief can be a species of idleness. The cure for grief is movement toward people, reaching out toward people with the richest qualities you have in you to give. You must learn to break down the wall of separateness that is the fence behind which the lonely person hides.

It may be helpful to remember the words of the British statesman Benjamin Disraeli, "Grief is the agony of an instant; the indulgence of grief the blunder of a lifetime."

On Morals

Is happiness a moral issue? I think so. I believe that every human being has a moral responsibility to be happy, and to share happiness with others. I believe it is completely immoral to be unhappy. I believe it is immoral for people who think they are moral and want to change people to be like them, to act, think, and live like them.

The prophets of happiness see life as it is, a far healthier view than the dreary moralists of gloom who want to make people good rather than happy. The point is you can't be good unless you are happy. And since happiness is internal, it means you are happiness. You have a responsibility to live it and to share it with others; and the more you give, the more you have. The dreary moralists don't give; they take away from the pure joy of living, and in that context, they are immoral.

These are the words of Robert Louis Stevenson, "If your morals make you dreary, depend upon it they are wrong." He didn't mean that if your life seems dull that you must abandon moral standards and seek happiness by stepping on other people's toes or on your own toes with indulgence and indolence. To live by fear, intimidation, frustration, and indecision is immoral to the extent that it makes you your little self, living in a dungeon you create for yourself. To live with the joy of life every twenty-four hours is another way of expressing love for others and for yourself, respect for others and for yourself. To me, this is creative morality.

Here is a thought to live by, written by George Bernard Shaw, "What is morality? Gentility."

The Barbershop Quartet

In San Diego, I went to a barbershop to have my shoes shined. I sat down and listened to the talk around me. A quartet of men were singing the praises of their cars.

"I have a Chevvy, a beauty. It's done close to 30,000 miles and no trouble."

"Mine's done over 40,000."

"How often do you get the oil changed?"

"Oh, I don't know, maybe every 2,000 miles. How about you?"

"I don't think that's enough, pal. I get mine changed every 1,000 miles. Filter every 3,000 to 5,000. That's the way to keep your car in good shape."

"I don't know. My car's done over 60,000, and I change the oil every 1,200 to 1,300 miles."

"You take care of your car; it'll take care of you."

The four men kept talking, two getting haircuts, two cutting hair. The shoeshine fellow and I just listened.

I thought to myself, "These fellows seem to know cars—and there's nothing wrong with that—but do they know anything at all about self-image? They look to be about thirty-five to forty-five, all of them, but do they practice creative living? They apparently like to be good citizens; they are all shaved, they keep their hair cut neatly, they oil their cars, they probably spend Sunday mornings washing their cars down so that the metal sparkles. Their cars will certainly get them where they want to go, but do they believe in other positive goals each day? Do they see a glistening self-image, or have they lost it in their fight for money and status and in their exclusive absorption in cars and such?" George Bernard Shaw said, "Better keep yourself clean and bright; you are the window through which you see the world." I say, "Better keep your self-image clean and bright. It is the window through which you see the world."

Most of us, regrettably, take better care of our cars than we do of the image of ourselves, which disappears somewhere—and with it goes our drive for happiness. What is your daily goal? Do you strive for creative living and self-fulfillment, steering your mind to productive, useful goals? If you try, try, try, you'll never have an energy crisis. You will have all the mental and spiritual fuel necessary to reach your destination.

The Small Potato

Carlyle said, "Society is founded on hero worship." We see it expressed dramatically in our lives. We cheer the winner in a prizefight, the actress for a memorable performance. We cheer our favorite football or baseball team and shout for joy when they are the winners of the season.

We love a winner because we love ourselves; and vicariously, we put ourselves in the place of the successful man, dreaming and hoping that someday, it will be our turn to be cheered and applauded for outstanding achievement.

We all have our hearts set on success, naturally. We persevere, believing that the day will come when we will reach our goal. Yet by the very nature of things, man is a paradox. He performs various acts daily that are inconsistent with achieving importance. He persists in doing the very things that will make him unimportant—the very things that will make him a small potato—and he takes all the time in the world to become insignificant.

All of us, more or less, receive little wounds from people in the daily struggle for contentment, and we exaggerate their significance by brooding over them. These wounds become so great to us, though unimportant, that they make us insignificant for the time we spend coddling them, thereby wounding ourselves more in the process.

Many of us are so concerned with the business of being a small potato, I thought it would be of value to jot down what to do and what not to do about it. With practice, you can become a small potato indeed.

Coddle your regrets. Let your mind continue to long for what has passed. Complain and be discontented when things go wrong at the time you expected the reverse. Forget that contentment should be your first step to progress. Be petty about your neighbor's good fortune. Stay hurt and disappointed about small matters.

Don't stop brooding over a grievance. Don't devote your time to worthwhile actions and feelings. Don't dare to think of a great thought, of wonderful affection, or of a lasting undertaking. Don't remember that every scrap of time is worth saving. Don't remember that you are here for a few decades at best and that life is too short to be a small potato.

Follow these precepts carefully, and I can assure you that you will become the smallest of the small potatoes.

You Can't Retire From Life

When I was in medical school, more than fifty years ago, a fellow student named Mickey was hospitalized with a severe case of influenza. He almost died from the disease, which was a much more serious problem then than it is today.

He recovered partially, and his condition was no longer critical, but his recovery was not complete. My fellow students and I would visit him at the hospital; it was extremely depressing. Formerly husky and energetic, with bristling blond hair, Mickey was pale, had lost much weight, and he still looked sick. His skin was colorless, his eyes were somber. You felt when you saw him that he envied you your health. My friends and I felt uncomfortable talking to him at his bedside, but we took turns visiting him.

Then one day, there was a sign on his closed door: NO VISITORS. We were alarmed, but there was no cause. Mickey's life was not in danger.

Mickey had asked the doctor to put up the sign. The visits of his friends and relatives had not cheered him. Instead, they had made him feel more glum. He wanted nothing to do with us. Later, Mickey told us how he felt during these days when he wanted nothing to do with the world of people. He felt scornful toward everybody and everything. He felt that each of us was worthless or ridiculous as a person. He told us that, in the prison of his mind, no one escaped the lash of his criticism. He just wanted to be left alone with the misery of his thoughts. There was no pleasure in him. Depressed by his physical deterioration, he felt a rejection of life growing in him until he renounced the world.

These were truly days of no-pleasure for Mickey. His resentment was too great for him to tolerate.

But he was lucky.

The day nurse, understanding his state of mind, decided to help him.

One day, after some tricky preludes, she told him that there was a girl patient who was suffering emotionally; Mickey could lift her spirits if he would write her love letters. Mickey wrote her one letter, then two. He pretended that he had seen her briefly one day and that he had thought about her ever since. After they were both well, he suggested, in a note, perhaps they could take walks in the park together.

Mickey felt pleasure in writing these letters—for the first time in many days—and his health began to improve. He wrote many letters and was soon walking spiritedly around the room. Soon, he was to be discharged from the hospital.

This knowledge saddened him because he had never seen the girl. So much pleasure had been derived from writing of his adoration, and a glow of love would come to his face at the thought of her. But he had never seen her—not even once!

Mickey asked the nurse if he could visit the girl in her room. The nurse approved and gave him the room number—414.

But there was no such room. There was no such girl.

And Mickey learned the truth—that the nurse had done her best to make him well. Seeing his gloom, sensing his critical, hating thoughts toward everyone, she felt that to recover from his illness, he needed pleasure in his life. She sensed that what Mickey needed to give him pleasure was the opportunity to give to a fellow patient, a fellow sufferer. She told him about the imaginary girl, and that turned the tide of his emotions.

So, Mickey left the hospital wiser, knowing in his heart the futility of resentment—and the happiness one gets from giving. He told us the story, for we were once again his friends. Mickey told it to us contentedly. His eyes gleamed, his cheeks were aglow, because he knew how it felt to escape from the dark world of self-inflicted gloom into the sunny world where one can live with pleasure.

Remember the words of John Donne:

> ***Despair is the damp of hell, as***
> ***joy is the serenity of heaven.***

Our Good Earth

Paul B. Sears, the distinguished naturalist, said, "This is our world."

In these four short words, he expressed man's responsibility throughout the ages to do something to really mean this is our world. Man evolves as a better human being when he realizes his responsibility to come to terms with nature, with his fellow men, and with himself. However, he must come to happy term with himself before he can accomplish anything constructive with others and with the outside world. The three worlds in which he lives—the world of his body, his mind, and his spirit—are his good earth. He cannot come to terms with nature if he doesn't come to terms with himself. He cannot be a friend to others or nature unless he is a friend to himself. He must save his own existence from destructive forces before he can talk about preserving the life of being in the forest. He must control the violence within him before he can control the violence around him. He must control the pollution in his mind and spirit control the garbage of hurt feelings before he can control the pollution of air and water. Wars and the hydrogen bomb have taught us that we can die together. Even though no workable formula has been devised to show us how to live together, we can each make a start right now by doing something about the dignity crisis, respecting our personal dignity and the dignity of others, understanding our personal needs and the personal needs of others.

On Wishful Thinking

Wishful thinking is a form of daydreaming. When we cannot stand up to the tensions of reality, when we make a temporary compromise by walking away from truth, we think we are sustaining ourselves through passive inaction, and we hope that things will turn out the way we want. Of course, this never happens, because daydreaming or wishful thinking accomplishes nothing. Sooner or later, we have to return to reality, adjust to it in a creative way, and accept daily living as a challenge, not as a compromise. Wishful thinking is a compromise that doesn't work satisfactorily for anyone.

You cannot compromise with creative thinking. You cannot compromise even with destructive thinking. Which shall it be? Constructive or destructive? You can make the choice, but you can't use daydreaming in the process.

There is nothing wrong with daydreaming now and then for a few moments or hours if it is used as relaxation from tension. Then you recall happy moments, successful moments in the past to renew your energies for the present.

Miguel de Unamuno said, "To think is to converse with oneself." But will this conversation be productive or unproductive? When you converse with yourself, you must play ball with yourself to find the big you. Only then will you be able to converse with others. When you are a friend to yourself, you will be a friend to others. And you cannot be a friend to yourself by inadequate thinking, by wishful thinking, or by daydreaming. As we say, think creatively, then do creatively. When? Now! Is this our world or isn't it?

Fishing

Many years ago, I had a yacht that I used for fishing; but I must confess I never caught a fish on any weekend during any season.

If the truth were known, I got rid of the yacht because I found a simple way of catching fish—and I don't mean by buying them in a fish store. I was sitting on my terrace one sunny afternoon. I held a string in my right hand about a foot long. It was dangling in the air when I conjured up the idea I was fishing. I will pass this idea on to you because you do not need a yacht, a smaller craft, or a boat at all to go fishing. Moreover, you do not need a rod and reel, a hook, or bait. All you need is a string, any string, a foot or less in length.

You sit in a chair anywhere, and you suspend the string from your hand as if you are angling for symbolic fish. As you wait to catch the fish, you will have time to reflect, which you can seldom do during the hectic activity of the day. Reflection means relaxation, when you have the opportunity to take stock of yourself, to see if it is possible to do something for yourself and be a better person for tomorrow. And this you can do.

Just think of a moment when your mind was distorted by a destructive emotion like anger. Perhaps you are going through the throes of it now. Notice how it makes you see red. You forget how useless such waste of energy really is. You forget that in hurting someone else, you have accomplished nothing except to hurt yourself. If such a wasteful emotion is devouring you, hold on to that string in your hand. Wait patiently. If you do, you may not actually grab a fish, but you will be able to do something far more important; you will be able to grab hold of yourself. Try it!

Number "65"

The book *Life Begins at Forty* helped lift the ceiling on worrying about age, like a moratorium on debts, but the number sixty-five remains a deadly number. This is partly a socioeconomic factor. Many business corporations, feeling sixty-five symbolizes the end of a person's value as a producer, have established this age as one of compulsory retirement. At any rate, sixty-five is not a number to ring out in musical chimes; it may soon threaten the status of thirteen as the unmentionable numeral. Many people, at sixty-five, tell themselves that life is over. They think constantly about death and dwell on physical symptoms that could cause death. Each day becomes a delaying action against the forces of death instead of a dedication to enjoying life. Their thoughts brim over with fear, and their conversation is a recital of the deaths and illnesses of friends and relatives.

Worry sweeps around in their minds like pigeons descending upon breadcrumbs, and they spend the rest of their years living with death.

Others reach sixty-five and collapse in a kind of rosy inertia. They have, they feel, reached the sunshine years and are entitled to complete retirement. They want to sleep at night and take catnaps during the day; they want to lie in their beds at night and occupy deck chairs in the daytime. Their attitude toward everything is horizontal, never vertical. They will not walk, they will ride in cars; they will not do, they will rest. They will not even think; TV or the newspapers will do their thinking for them! Surely after the years of struggle, making money to pay the bills, raising children, the retirement years must be glorious. The number sixty-five is deadly to these people They—is it you?—waste their time fearing death, since death is a natural process that they can do nothing about. They—is it you?—will not enjoy retirement from life; it is a premature death.

Some younger people—is it you?—dissipate their productive energies with worry over what will happen to them when they come face to face with age sixty-five.

While you have the privilege of life on this earth, and it is a privilege, in spite of unceasing problems you should live. You should live, whether you are sixteen or sixty-five. Be like Ezio Pinza, an inspiration to millions when he starred in *South Pacific,* reaching the peak of his career at an age when some people retire. Pinza was young when others his age force themselves to decay; he was far younger in spirit than some less fortunate people in their early twenties. Naturally, older age requires a person to place sensible limits on his physical capabilities. When you are older, you can't run around like a young kid and, if you have a heart condition, you must further restrict your activities. Yet, the older person has qualities that the child or adolescent hasn't even begun to develop.

The main point is: IN OLDER AGE, EACH DAY CAN BE THRILLING. It's really up to the individual. It's up to you. Still, if you are over sixty-five and have already wasted time moping, stop blaming yourself. You're not perfect, no one is, and self-blame will not help you. You must have self-respect as long as you live. So live creatively every day of your life.

When Pablo Casals reached ninety-five, a young reporter threw him a question, "Mr. Casals, you are ninety-five and the greatest cellist that ever lived. Why do you still practice six hours a day?" And Mr. Casals answered, "Because I think I'm making progress."

Your goal is to make progress every day of your life.

Frustration

How can you overcome frustration?

Everyone experiences one kind of frustration or another every day. Frustration should stimulate us, help us solve a problem, not yield to it. When we are crushed under it, it becomes a chronic type of negative feeling.

We become creative artists when we let our servomechanism create ideas and solve problems. But too many of us jam our creative mechanism with worry, anxiety, and fear, trying to force a solution with the forebrain, the seat of our thinking but not the seat of doing. This jamming of the creative servomechanism doesn't serve us at all. It inhibits us from our goals, putting a roadblock of negation in front of us, creating frustration.

There are five roadblocks of frustration:

1. We worry not only before making a decision but after. We carry this extra fifty pounds of worry on our minds all day.

   The cure? Express anxiety before we make a decision—not after. There are, let us say, five solutions to a problem. Anxiety is creative while we choose which road to take. Once we choose, however, we must stop worrying and call upon the confidence of past successes to guide us in the present. If we call upon the failures of the past to guide us in the present, we create immediate frustration.

2. We not only worry and fret about today, we worry about yesterday and tomorrow. This sets up a pattern of instant frustration because we call upon past failures and future apprehensions to guides us in the present. We can't think positively with negative feelings.

   The cure? Think only of today. Every day is a complete lifetime. Forget yesterday; lose it in the vacuum of time. Tomorrow doesn't exist; when it comes it is another day. Let your servomechanism do what it can do well; respond to the present. Try, try, try—now, now, now.

3. We try to do too many things at one time. This creates tension of tone, spasm instead of comfort. When we try to do too many things at one time, we try to do the impossible.

The cure? Don't fight relaxation. Join it. Learn to do one thing at a time. This brings relaxation. This frees you from the burden of hurry and failure.

4. We wrestle with our problems twenty-four hours a day without letup. We carry our problems from the job, to the home, to our bed. This creates tension that produces frustration.

The cure? Sleep on your problem if you are unable to solve it. Sleep on it, not with it. Let your success mechanism work for you when you hit the pillow as you recall past successes.

5. We refuse to relax. We don't know what it is. We just know the word, that's all. The spasm of repeated worry produces the spasm of frustration. You can't have someone relax for you. You've got to do it on your own.

The cure? You sit in a room of your mind, and you relax there to cut the electric circuit of distress.

Relaxation overcomes frustration. Don't think it. Work for it. Do it—now!

Remember these words of Plato:

Nothing in the affairs of men is worth worrying about.

Courtesy

Laurence Sterne said, "Hail the small sweet courtesies of life, for smooth do they make the road of it."

What is courtesy? It is the beginning of friendship. It is the beginning of an open mind, when you realize that all people are children of God and that they deserve the same consideration and treatment that you expect yourself. It is the will to succeed through a gesture, a little thing. Life is full of little things that make it big and worthwhile, when we overcome small pains and petty grievances that little remedies like courtesy can cure.

Courtesy is thoughtfulness and consideration for the feelings of others as well as your own. It is caring put to use. Courtesy is a smile turned into a creative performance. When expressed, it increases the well-being of all concerned.

The small blows to our respect and integrity, the small jolts to our sense of worth, cause an incredible number of heartaches in the world.

What is courtesy? It is the goodwill you offer another human being. And more. It is goodwill that you offer to yourself, better health to yourself. Could you express courtesy and at the same time feel angry, inferior, uncertain, frustrated, or empty? No, of course not. When you express courtesy, you see the big self in others and feel it in yourself.

Think of courtesy as an important goal that automatically creates empathy for others and for yourself.

Garbage Disposal

A secretary who works in an advertising agency comes home from work every evening, feeds her poodle, then herself. After dinner, she looks at herself in the mirror for a while, pulls out a straying hair from her eyebrow, makes up her lashes, then gives her lips a dab of lipstick. She runs a comb through her short, cropped hair and sweeps a few of the graying strands along to their proper place. After eyeing herself with a final critical gaze, she moves toward the door. The poodle is accustomed to this routine because it happens the same way at the same time every day. He watches her open and close the door behind her.

She walks down the steps, through the door down below, down the stone stairs to the street, where she stops beside a garbage can to deposit the paper bag full of garbage she has carried with her. Then, she looks around toward the end of the street, facing the park as though she were expecting to see someone. With finality, she walks up the steps to her apartment where the poodle is waiting near the door.

Her neighbors don't know why she grooms herself just to dispose of the garbage. The fact is she hopes that one of these days, her husband, an army chaplain, will return. He had been reported missing in action years ago. She sometimes thinks there is no hope, yet she clings to hope. Therefore, she clings to tidiness, orderliness, attractiveness.

Recently, a writer on her return from Europe criticized New York as being the filthiest city in the world, with garbage all over the place. However, travel should have shown her that all cities, particularly the large ones, have problems with garbage disposal, and they all make efforts to meet these problems. Human beings should make an effort to dispose of personal garbage, too. I don't mean the garbage in the house; I mean the garbage in the mind. We all have it to a lesser or greater degree. Mental garbage is the waste that piles up from indolence and indecision, from fear and resentment. These destructive traits clog up the mind, with refuse and easily infect and fatigue the spirit.

It is very easy to groom yourself like the lady in this story; it is just as easy now and then to clean the house of your mind by symbolically taking hold of the garbage of hurt feelings, throwing it into a receptacle—the past—and walking away from it forever.

Mañana Incorporated

Are you a member of Mañana Incorporated? "Mañana" in Spanish means "tomorrow," and Mañana Incorporated is an organization that leaves things undone until tomorrow. It is the world's largest organization, with more members than any religious, political, philosophical, or industrial organization. To join, you must cling to one glaring fault: the tendency to put things off until "tomorrow." Millions slavishly follow this blueprint for failure for a lifetime.

Colleges give no courses in it because it's too easy and does not lead to advancement.

This doesn't mean that we should not learn the art of leisure, which is totally different. Idle people have the least leisure, because leisure is the reward of work. It feeds the body and mind to meet the demands of tomorrow. As Thoreau said, "He employs true leisure who has time to improve his soul's estate." The man who leaves things for tomorrow hasn't time to improve anything, and uselessness is emptiness.

Mañana Incorporated espouses a philosophy of failure, because no one has ever seen tomorrow. We indulge in wishful thinking when we dream that tomorrow will be free of trouble. However, we can constructively plan for tomorrow, looking for ways to better ourselves instead of tying ourselves to techniques that will leave us marking time, wallowing in a vacuum.

Every day we must strive to break away from our membership in Mañana Incorporated. We must break away from the oppressive hold of fear and worry that makes us lazy and say, "Well, we'll take care of that detail tomorrow." We must send in our letter of resignation.

Say to yourself every day, "I will do something better tomorrow. I will improve myself tomorrow, and I will try to be more sincere with others and with myself." But more important, forget about tomorrow until it gets here. Start improving yourself *today, now, this very minute!*

Listen to the words of Horace (65-8 B.C.), "Cease to inquire what the future has in store, and take as a gift Whatever the day brings forth."

How To Shadowbox

Shadowboxing is one of the arts necessary in the career of the boxer. It teaches him poise, agility, and grace: how to shift quickly with his feet as he dances away from his opponent. In a way, shadowboxing is a modified form of dancing.

I always think of the ballet dancer as a person who, avoiding an enemy, pirouettes and flies through the air, then disappears. I have one concrete example to prove my point. Many years ago, I operated on a patient for an injured nose. He was known as the Coca-Cola kid, who with amazing fancy footwork considered to be a form of shadowboxing—danced right out of Hungary, away from the enemy behind the Iron Curtain, and into an American audience.

We should all train ourselves in a form of shadowboxing for the battles we have to fight every day. The kind of shadowboxing I mean will give agility, grace, and quick movement to *your mind* so that it can avoid or overpower its greatest enemy—*laziness*. Laziness can destroy us faster than a Firpo, faster than a Johnson, a Sharkey, a Fitzsimmons, a Tunney, a Dempsey, a Marciano, or a Mohammed Ali.

All you have to do to become a champion is to shadowbox for a few minutes every morning when you get up. You stand in front of the mirror and you shadowbox. You are fighting laziness; you can outsmart him, you can tire him out, he can't keep up with your creative thinking. You outmaneuver him. Laziness is not going to stand in the way of your victory. Give him the old one, two. Make laziness a has-been. Don't be defeated by a worthless opponent.

Remember the words from the Bible (Proverbs, XXIII:21):

Drowsiness [laziness] shall clothe a man with rags.

Blackout

I was one of millions inconvenienced by the power failure years ago that crippled a huge area on the eastern coast of the United States. My lights were out; my phone was dead. I lit a candle and located my transistor radio, learning that nine states were hit; thirty million people in darkness.

The blackout occurred about 5:30 P.M. I had to catch a 9 A.M. plane for California the following morning; I was scheduled to lecture.

The lightless night passed, hour upon dark hour. I went to bed early, but I could not sleep. I argued with myself.

"Why worry? No one can blame you for not going. Go next week."

"No, I was looking forward to lecturing, and I'm going."

It was like a tennis match. I batted the ball back and forth. At 3:30 A.M. the lights were still out; the elevator was still dead. Living on the eighteenth floor was no advantage in this situation.

Finally, I decided that I was going toward my goal. I dressed, grabbed a hat, coat, my two grips, and a candle. I opened the door to the stairway. In candlelight, I dimly saw stairs, stairs, and more stairs below me.

Then I dropped the candle and saw nothing at all.

What to do? In a wave of negativism, I told myself to go back to my apartment and give up on what I wanted. But my big-self overcame these negative thoughts, and I proceeded toward my goal. Step by step, I inched my way down to the seventeenth floor, walking slowly, carefully, then down to the sixteenth, the fifteenth, the fourteenth… down to the street. When I stood on New York's still dark sidewalks, I dropped my luggage with a thud. I felt as if I had just released a couple of five-hundred-pound weights. I was partway to my goal; I still had to get a taxi to take me to the airport. I stumbled around, waving my hands. Getting a taxi seemed impossible.

I figured a cab would need an hour to get to the airport. At 7:55, a taxi stopped for me—just in time. Departure time for the plane was 9 A.M.

I turned my back to pick up my luggage, and then saw the taxi moving off without me.

After my first reaction of anger, I felt despair. "I did my best," I told myself. "I'll go back to sleep."

"No," my big-self urged, "you can still make it." And I did. A responsible cab driver picked me up. He took a few seasoned shortcuts and drove swiftly and safely. I made the plane. Hours later, I was in San Francisco, then Monterey. I enjoyed speaking, enjoyed my trip—more so because I had not blacked out with the city.

I felt good because, in the battle in my mind between success and failure instincts, my success instincts had won, and I had not let adverse circumstances keep me from my goal.

My story is illustrative, not an exercise in self-praise. Truthfully, I have failed myself many, many times in my life. Still, even as I grow older, I feel happy that I am not falling into the nonliving blackout that crushes so many people. In harnessing my active, goal-oriented success instincts, I strengthen my enjoyment of life all the time. The blackout affected thirty million people for a short time—blackout beyond human control. Emotional blackouts crush millions more every day—and often for a lifetime—a blackout we can control if we remember we came into this world to succeed, not to fail.

You must resist the emotional blackout of negative feelings that keep you from living creatively. You can move out of an emotional blackout into brightness and hope.

Here is a thought to live by, by Thomas Fuller (1608-1681), "It is always darkest just before the day dawneth."

The Stock Market

Many of us play the stock market because we live in hope that we'll strike it rich sooner or later and profit enough to hoard for a rainy day when we can take it easy, travel, live a leisurely life. So we listen to tips on the market whenever they come, from wherever they come. We want to believe that what we hear is true, hopeful that we will make money to fulfill a dream.

I am acquainted with one professional who knows the market thoroughly. He can sense oncoming fluctuations in the stocks with uncanny accuracy. When I go to meet him on a Sunday at noon at a restaurant for lunch, I prepare myself. By that, I mean I sit to his right or to his left, but never on the other side of the table. He was never convincing when I sat opposite him. Before, during, and after lunch, he would glare at me as if possessed. The veins in his bald head would bulge, and he would tell me about the eccentricities of the stock market. To convince me thoroughly, he would tug violently on my sleeve to punctuate his remarks. Strange as it may seem, most of the time, he is right, though I must confess he occasionally pulls a real boner.

I pride myself as an expert also; but I am an expert in another kind of stock. I am an expert in mental and spiritual stock. Happily, the tips I can give you are always good. I never make a mistake like my friend, and I don't have to pull at your coat sleeve. The stocks I speak about are blue-chip; they never go down; they always go up, and the dividends are regular and more than gratifying. The stocks of which I speak are charity, understanding, courage, and self-respect. They are the success stocks. Invest in them, and you'll never go wrong. This is a sure tip. You are bound to make a handsome profit.

Take A Bow

The custom of bowing has existed since the beginning of civilization, and many schools of thought have existed in different countries on how to bow. Every country, depending on custom and tradition, has its own method and preference. History tells us about the French musketeer bowing low and gracefully before his lady, sweeping his multicolored plumed hat to the ground. It tells us of the Italian courtier of the Renaissance who bowed more carefully with studied precision as he paid his respects to Lorenzo de Medici. History points out a romantic variation when Sir Walter Raleigh lowered his cape to the wet earth and, bowing, helped Queen Elizabeth I across the path. History gives a variety of methods, including the Siamese courtiers who knelt and bowed their heads to the ground before their emperor.

As many ways as there are of bowing, there are that many reasons for doing so. A slave long ago bowed low out of fear. And those of us who pray today bow not out of fear but out of reverence, out of faith. Once, we bowed out of loyalty to a king; but times have changed, and in our democratic way of life, it would be a rare occurrence for a laborer to bow before the President of the United States. Both would be embarrassed. People from all walks of life shake hands. We have dispensed with fear, with feathers, with frills, and with finery when we bow; and that maneuver or act is essentially relegated to receiving praise.

Praise is a useful ingredient in our daily routine. It indicates accomplishment in one form or another. Praise is what an actress, a violinist, a singer needs at the end of the performance.

Even though self-praise is no recommendation, there is a time now and then when you can indulge in it. Then you should take a bow, not for the great things you did but for the many things you did *not do.*

You should take a bow because you did not worship such a false god as greed. You did not strangle your enemy even though an inclination was there. You did not steal. You did not speak ill of your neighbor. You were not envious of your friend's success; or, if you were, you concealed your envy until you yourself were no longer aware of it.

Take a bow, good person. You deserve it.

Five Minutes Can Change Your Life

I have asked you before, and I ask you again to give yourself five minutes of the day to walk into a room in your mind. Of course, this is an imaginary room. You should imagine you are sitting in a chair, and as you look outside the window, you see a geyser letting off steam. This is a symbol for you to let go of the tensions that have oppressed you during the day.

You must take stock of yourself. You have assets and liabilities. Your liabilities are fear, loneliness, resentment, and uncertainty. Your assets are faith, understanding, compassion, self-respect.

Your liabilities, the destructive emotions, are the deadly poisons that infect you within. They disfigure your self-image. Your never-ending doubt or fear is a never-ending spasm, corrosion, a never-ending paralysis. Your resentment may abuse someone else but will abuse you most of all.

On the other hand, the assets of your built-in success mechanism enhance not only someone else's image but also your own.

As Tolstoy put it, "Faith is the force of life." Spend five minutes a day finding out who you are. Discover that your assets are there for you to use, that you have a moral responsibility to do so. Let the improvement of your self-image five minutes a day be your personal faith in your worth, urging you to rise to your full stature of dignity to become the big you—the you that you really are. Make this your daily goal for as long as you live: to change your life for the better.

The Itch

The itch, no matter where it occurs, is a cutaneous irritation usually followed by uncontrollable scratching, and the performance of the fingers has all sorts of variations depending on the severeness of the itch and the physical and mental condition of the individual. For example, a vigorous truck driver will tackle the itch quite differently from a fragile schoolteacher. He will apply force to relieve it while she will approach it as if she were slowly turning a page of a book.

There are various gradations between the rough and the delicate approach—the staccato peck or the lingering, procrastinating stroke, the fastidious scrape or the tender, indulgent pat, the angry scratch or the exhilarating tickle. And, depending on personal preference, there may or may not be a vocal accompaniment.

An itchy area of skin can erupt with a rash caused by a severer form of irritation from the outside world or from within; but the usual itch is not accompanied by such manifestation. All itches are destructive, even if only in a minor way and even if the itch is purely a mental one. We all now and then get the itch to run away from trouble; but the itch I should like to speak of is constructive, and it is worthwhile getting it now and then. To travel away from trouble is futile. It leads nowhere, for you must have a point of departure and return before you go.

The best itch to get is the itch that reaches the mind and the soul— the constructive itch; the itch to improve yourself. Don't be stagnant and lethargic; don't be smug and satisfied with yourself. Sit down and take stock of your assets and liabilities now and then. Build your assets, lessen your liabilities. You surely have learned that it is good to get a physical checkup once a year. Get the itch to check yourself mentally and spiritually at least once a year. You don't need a physician for it; you can do it yourself.

Remember the words of Plautus, "To mean well is nothing without to do well."

Expect A Miracle

One Sunday, I drove from Salinas, California, to San Jose—approximately sixty miles away—to speak at a church. Time was running short, and we didn't know the road too well. *"Only a miracle will get me there on time,"* I said to myself.

One minute before the services started, I walked into the paster's office, and we both sighed in relief. Behind his chair, I saw a sign. It read, EXPECT A MIRACLE.

All of us suffer occasionally from the feeling of frustration and despair and feel that we are unlucky, that we just cannot get a break in life. I do not believe that there is anyone who doesn't, once in a while, feel that way. At such times all of us can use a miracle, or the expectation of a miracle.

You have every right to expect a miracle—every right to feel that a miracle is forthcoming—not in a literal sense, of course, because no one should expect miraculous intervention on his behalf.

Your miracle must come from inside yourself. It must come from your faith in yourself no matter how trying the pressures. It must come from your attitude of determination in crises, as you turn crises into creative opportunities. It must come from the support you give yourself in all circumstances.

The miracle you should and must welcome is your self-acceptance.

Your acceptance of your weaknesses.

Your acceptance of your strengths.

Your acceptance of your imperfections.

Once you accept yourself, you can give yourself help that is little short of miraculous.

Personality

Can personality be changed? Of course!

Remember, you are made up of liabilities and assets. You have within you the desire to be happy and unhappy, the will to succeed and the will to fail, the desire for self-fulfillment, and the desire for self-destruction. When you look in the mirror, you will find two different people at two different times. Sometimes, you will have a frown on your face and feel frustrated; sometimes, you will have a smile on your face because you feel successful. When you like the better you, you are at that moment enlarging the scope of your personality. If you choose frustration as a way of life, you undermine your personality and make your image shrink. In other words, you and you alone can add to your assets or accumulate more liabilities. No one else can do this for you. Here are some points you can utilize to be the better on, the big you, with a better personality.

1. Do one thing at a time, shoot for one goal at a time.
2. Live in the present. Live today.
3. Forget the mistakes of yesterday. Yesterday has gone forever.
4. Stop criticizing yourself and stop criticizing others.
5. Yearn for self-improvement.
6. Hold on to your self-respect by appraising yourself honestly.
7. Learn to listen to others. It helps remove bias from your opinions.
8. If you have a goal, reach for it. If you make a mistake, try again.
9. Don't be timid in conversation. Talk even ff you make a mistake.
10. Exercise your imagination creatively to achieve success.

Remember the words of Charles Schwab, "Personality is to a man what perfume is to a flower."

Important You

Recognize your importance to yourself. You must realize that it is not egotism when you come to understand that you are the most important person in the world to yourself. It is not conceit or vanity or selfishness when you brush aside life's trivialities and irrelevancies to give your inner self the attention it deserves.

Important you! You must not interpret this narcissistically—that is, being in love with your image, absorbed in yourself to the exclusion of other people in this world. You should merely attune yourself to your possibilities, work patiently with yourself to grow and accept your growth—because you are important—and then you should go out to meet life, share with other people, try to make the world a warmer place. Daily practice will make you the important you that you really are; creating, when you need it, instant confidence.

When you spend your days building and building, trying and trying, emphasizing your emotional capacities over and over, increasing your confidence in yourself, accepting yourself, getting closer to yourself, what do you have? Important you.

Now and then, face the mirror and say to yourself, "No matter how tough things are, I'm with me! I shall spend time to make the most of each day, use it to give the greatest possible meaning to my life. This is what creative Psycho-Cybernetics is all about: becoming a professional human being, creating a new dimension in personal freedom, on my own terms."

Recognize the big you, the important you.

Remember the words of Epicterus, "He is a wise man who does not grieve for the things which he has not, but rejoices for those which he has."

Set Your Goal

Many of us feel that we have no goals, but that is far from the truth. The truth is that all of us have goals of various kinds; but one goal common to all is the desire to live and to be happy.

Millions of men and women waste much of their lives on small details that get them nowhere. We live fast, but to what purpose, to what end? We get nowhere, and we do it on the double. We are not able to simplify our lives by remembering our generic goal—to be happy. And you can't rush after happiness, not because happiness is elusive but because when you run after it, you are running away from it. Why? You must remember that happiness is internal. You are happiness, and you can't run after it when it is already within you.

You must be realistic and live creatively instead of running around a vicious cycle of nothingness. If people who run around as if they don't know what they want would stop to think a moment, they would know what they want. Then slowly, without rushing, they would work for it and live for it. Remember, *live creatively instead of quickly.*

You don't have to take to the woods and forget it all. Take to yourself, resolve within yourself what goal you want to achieve, cut out the useless details that take you away from yourself. Then go after your goal with thought, determination, and belief, a goal within your capabilities and training.

You go forward toward your goals when:

1. You reach for today's opportunities.
2. You exercise your right to succeed.
3. You use your courage to stand up under stress.
4. You jump the hurdles of doubt and indecision.
5. You are aware of your real potential

6. You see yourself as successful
7. You seek improvement.
8. You nourish your self-image with faith and belief.

Here is a thought to live by: "Be ashamed to die until you have won some goal for yourself and for others."

Joy In An Active Life

THERE IS JOY IN THE ACTIVE LIFE FOR ALL OF ONE'S LIFE.

A goal every day is important, something to move toward in this pulsating world. It is terrible to throw away your years sitting around moping, feeling sorry for yourself. The idea of escaping into your mind now and then to relax a bit when you need it and I believe most people do—is not at all inconsistent with this active philosophy of doing and moving.

The person who lives creatively will stay in the swim of things, will be busy and interested and involved—and will be able to clear an hour or two relaxing, escaping to a room of his mind to let go of tension. He will be able to rebound from life's hard knocks.

Baseball player Larry Brown of the Cleveland Indians came back from a fractured skull that he suffered in a collision with another player to play hall again less than seven weeks later.

Entertainer Sammy Davis, Jr., was in the headlines a number of years ago after his crippling accident, but since then, he has come back stronger than ever as one of America's most versatile performers.

Poet Robert Frost, honored on his seventy-fifth birthday years ago by the U.S. Senate, was at first ignored in his own country. It was in England that he had his first poems published, then he came home and started on the road to renown.

You, too, may have to rebound—many times—from many troubles. To live creatively, you will have to keep pace with life and stay young.

An occasional retreat may help you.

Then back to living—not only when times are easy, but when times are tough.

The greatest joy in an active life is standing up to stress, rising above a problem, a misfortune, a blunder.

Here is what Jonathan Swift said, "May you live all the days of your life."

About Maxwell Maltz, M.D.

Dr. Maxwell Maltz (March 10, 1889–April 7, 1975) was an American cosmetic surgeon who created his self-improvement phenomenon, Psycho-Cybernetics, at age 61, after an already varied, colorful, and exceptionally successful career as a surgeon, writer, and speaker. Published in 1960, *Psycho-Cybernetics* has sold over 30 million copies since its original printing and remains a classic of self-help, self-improvement, and personal development.

According to Dr. Maltz, the process of psycho-cybernetics consists of steering your mind to productive, useful goals so you can reach peace of mind. In *Psycho-Cybernetics* and all the books that followed, Dr. Maltz speaks to the importance of a healthy self-image that is the roadmap to creating a better quality of life.

Dr. Maltz was inspired to move from treating "outer scars" to "inner scars" after seeing some patients' continuing to have feelings of unhappiness, unworthiness as well as personal insecurities that were not cured through cosmetic surgery, even though they believed they would feel happy after he gave them the perfect new faces they desired.

Dr. Maltz first wrote of this discovery in his book *New Faces, New Futures*. In this groundbreaking book, he suggested that many people "see themselves" inaccurately, their perceptions distorted by unchallenged and often erroneous beliefs embedded in their subconscious minds. After a decade of counseling hundreds of patients with his evolving "success conditioning techniques," Dr. Maltz published his findings, in 1960, in the original *Psycho-Cybernetics*.

Psycho-Cybernetics became an instant bestseller and made Dr. Maltz one of the most in-demand motivational speakers throughout the 1960s and the early 1970s. He went on to amass a wealth of "case history" material and produced numerous seminars, workshops, radio broadcasts, and more than a dozen books, all applying Psycho-Cybernetics to different purposes, from business success to athletic achievement to sex life improvement.

We continue to make Dr. Maltz's timeless work available to new generations.

About Matt Furey

After winning both national and world titles in wrestling and martial arts competition, Matt Furey went on to become a best-selling fitness and self-development author. Some of his books include Combat Conditioning, Expect to Win–Hate to Lose, The Unbeatable Man and 101 Ways to Magnetize Money in Any Economy. Two of Furey's audiobooks, Theatre of the Mind and 101 Ways to Magnetize Money in Any Economy are Nightingale-Conant best-sellers.

Furey's pioneering ways in bodyweight exercise paved the way for an entire movement of functional fitness, and his latest breakthroughs and techniques in utilizing the principles of Psycho-Cybernetics are available to his coaching members. For information on coaching in Psycho-Cybernetics and Theatre of the Mind, go to psycho-cybernetics.com/coaching.

Since 2005, when Furey became president of the Psycho-Cybernetics Foundation, he has held seminars and coaching programs all over the world. Furey has coached athletes at virtually every level: middle and high school, collegiate, Olympic and professional. He also works with writers, speakers, entrepreneurs and many other professionals.

To contact Matt Furey about coaching, seminars, licensing or translation rights, visit psycho-cybernetics.com/coaching or send an email to wmattfurey11@gmail.com.

Free Video from the Psycho-Cybernetics Foundation

As a purchaser of this Psycho-Cybernetics book, you are eligible to receive a free video, How to Defeat the Failure Mechanism. This video introduces concepts that Matt Furey, President of the Psycho-Cybernetics Foundation, teaches to all his coaching clients on how you can overcome the pain and trauma of failure and defeat. To receive this free video, email Matt directly at mattfurey11@gmail.com.

Coaching Services

If you're looking to move to the next level in your daily use of Psycho-Cybernetics principles; if you want a coach to help you truly live the good life by creating a more powerful self-image, be sure to go to psycho-cybernetics.com/coaching and fill out the brief questionnaire.

A Note from the Publisher

Maxwell Maltz Books is a Dedicated Catalog within **Thought Works Books,** a division of Micro Publishing Media. MPM is an indie publisher with dedicated imprints for special interests. We know there is a lot of competition for entertainment and reading time and that it is often difficult to find what you are looking for. We have made it easier by aggregating titles together that have similar themes or wisdom.

We created Thought Works Books not only to house the Classic Maxwell Maltz library but to shine a spotlight on the topic of the power of the mind to change people's lives. Dr. Maltz was considered a major pioneer. if not the father, of the new thought movement in the early 1960s and his groundbreaking book *Psycho-Cybernetics* sold over 30 million copies since its first publication. It is still in print and can be purchased in an updated edition edited by Matt Furey.

We hope you will add all of Dr. Maltz's works to your library as we believe they will help you transform your life while helping you feel empowered while doing it.

You can find the entire list at: **www.maxwellmaltzbooks.com**

www.ingramcontent.com/pod-product-compliance
Lightning Source LLC
LaVergne TN
LVHW011421080426
835512LV00005B/184